Kapaun's Battle

By

Jeff Gress

3rd Coast Books, LLC
19790 Hwy. 105 W. Ste. 1318
Montgomery, Texas 77356

3rd Coast Books, LLC
19790 Hwy. 105 W. Ste. 1318
Montgomery, TX 77356

www.3rd CoastBooks.com

ISBNs
Perfect Binding (Print) 978-1-946743-48-0
eBook/Mobi 978-1-946743-49-7
eBook/ePub 978-1-946743-50-3

Publisher-Ron W. Mumford
Project Coordinator - Ian W. Gorman MBA, Co-Publisher
Editors - Ian W. Gorman MBA, Faye Walker, Ph.D.
Cover Artist - Kathleen J. Shields, Kathleen's Graphics
Text Designer - Kathleen J. Shields, Kathleen's Graphics
Video Trailer - Alex Gonzales
Marketing/PR - Pamela K. Ott

CONTENTS

ACKNOWLEDGMENTS

I would like to offer a special thanks to all the people who helped make this project possible; all the crew at **360 Studios Ltd.**, **Veteran's Green Projects**, **Veteran's Green Coffee**, Keith Barrows, Michael Dinco, Bharathi Kommana, Phillip Wayne Jones, Michael W. Malott, Huong [Laura] Vu, Sergio Santoro, Antonio Choice, Steve Boyle, Ethan Boyle, Tony Boldi, Ryan Kotula, Kenneth Dowers, Asahi, Julia Barrows, Cindy Villarreal, Donald DeNoyer, Nicholas Nathaniel, Jahquell Johnson, Veronica Lynne, Harold & Maria LaBonte, Adrian Combs, and all the men and women serving in the Marine Corps, Army, Navy, Air Force and the National Guard who risk their lives daily to defend our country. This is dedicated to the veterans.

— Jeff Gress

U.S. Army Medal of Honor
Presented Posthumously to Chaplain Emil J. Kapaun

April 11, 2013 (link to info https://obamawhitehouse.archives.gov/the-press-office/2013/04/11/remarks-president-presentation-medal-honor-chaplain-emil-j-kapaun-us-arm)

Chaplain (Father) Emil J. Kapaun   1st Calvary Division Patch

Remarks by President Obama at Posthumous Presentation of the Medal of Honor to Chaplain Emil J. Kapaun, U.S. Army

East Room-April 11, 2013

THE PRESIDENT: Good afternoon, everybody. Please have a seat. On behalf of Michelle and myself, welcome to the White House. Thank you, Chaplain.

This year, we mark the 60th anniversary of the end of the Korean War — a time when thousands of our prisoners of war finally came home after years of starvation and hardship and, in some cases, torture. And among the homecomings, one stood out.

A group of our POWs emerged carrying a large wooden crucifix, nearly four feet tall. They had spent months on it, secretly collecting firewood, carving it — the cross and the body — using radio wire for a crown of thorns. It was a tribute to their friend, their chaplain, their fellow prisoner who had touched their souls and saved their lives — Father Emil Kapaun.

This is an amazing story. Father Kapaun has been called a shepherd in combat boots. His fellow soldiers who felt his grace and his mercy called him a saint, a blessing from God. Today, we bestow another title on him — recipient of our nation's highest military decoration, the Medal of Honor. After more than six decades of working to make this Medal a reality, I know one of Father Kapaun's comrades spoke for a lot of folks here when he said, "it's about time."

Father, as they called him, was just 35 years old when he died in that hellish prison camp. His parents and his only sibling, his brother, are no longer with us. But we are extremely proud to welcome members of the Kapaun family — his nephews, his niece, their children — two of whom currently serve in this country's National Guard. And we are very proud of them.

We're also joined by members of the Kansas congressional delegation, leaders from across our armed forces, and representatives from the Catholic Church, which recognizes Father Kapaun as a "Servant of God." And we are truly humbled to be joined by men who served alongside him — veterans and former POWs from the Korean War.

Now, I obviously never met Father Kapaun. But I have a sense of the man he was because in his story I see reflections of my own grandparents and their values, the people who helped to raise me. Emil and my grandfather were both born in Kansas about the same time, both were raised in small towns outside of Wichita. They were part of that Greatest Generation — surviving the Depression, joining the Army, serving in World War II. And they embodied those heartland values of honesty and hard work, decency, and humility — quiet heroes determined to do their part.

For Father Kapaun, this meant becoming an Army chaplain — serving God and country. After the Communist invasion of South Korea, he was among the first American troops that hit the beaches and pushed their way north through hard mountains and bitter cold. In his understated Midwestern way, he wrote home, saying, "this outdoor life is quite the thing" — (laughter) — and "I prefer to live in a house once in a while." But he had hope, saying, "It looks like the war will end soon."

That's when Chinese forces entered the war with a massive surprise attack — perhaps 20,000 soldiers pouring down on a few thousand Americans. In the chaos, dodging bullets and explosions, Father Kapaun raced between foxholes, out past the front lines, and into no-man's land — dragging the wounded to safety.

When his commanders ordered an evacuation, he chose to stay — gathering the injured, tending to their wounds. When the enemy broke through and the combat was hand-to-hand, he carried on —

comforting the injured and the dying, offering some measure of peace as they left this Earth.

When enemy forces bore down, it seemed like the end — that these wounded Americans, more than a dozen of them, would be gunned down. But Father Kapaun spotted a wounded Chinese officer. He pleaded with this Chinese officer and convinced him to call out to his fellow Chinese. The shooting stopped and they negotiated a safe surrender, saving those American lives.

Then, as Father Kapaun was being led away, he saw another American — wounded, unable to walk, laying in a ditch, defenseless. An enemy soldier was standing over him, rifle aimed at his head, ready to shoot. And Father Kapaun marched over and pushed the enemy soldier aside. And then as the soldier watched, stunned, Father Kapaun carried that wounded American away.

This is the valor we honor today — an American soldier who didn't fire a gun, but who wielded the mightiest weapon of all, a love for his brothers so pure that he was willing to die so that they might live. And yet, the incredible story of Father Kapaun does not end there.

He carried that injured American, for miles, as their captors forced them on a death march. When Father Kapaun grew tired, he'd help the wounded soldier hop on one leg. When other prisoners stumbled, he picked them up. When they wanted to quit — knowing that stragglers would be shot — he begged them to keep walking.

In the camps that winter, deep in a valley, men could freeze to death in their sleep. Father Kapaun offered them his own clothes. They starved on tiny rations of millet and corn and birdseed. He somehow snuck past the guards, foraged in nearby fields, and returned with rice and potatoes. In desperation, some men hoarded food. He convinced them to share. Their bodies were ravaged by dysentery. He grabbed some rocks, pounded metal into pots and boiled clean water. They lived in filth. He washed their clothes and he cleansed their wounds.

The guards ridiculed his devotion to his Savior and the Almighty. They took his clothes and made him stand in the freezing cold for hours. Yet, he never lost his faith. If anything, it only grew stronger. At night, he slipped into huts to lead prisoners in prayer, saying the Rosary, administering the sacraments, offering three simple words: "God bless you." One of them later said that with his very presence he could just for a moment turn a mud hut into a cathedral.

That spring, he went further — he held an Easter service. I just met with the Kapaun family. They showed me something extraordinary — the actual stole, the purple vestment that Father Kapaun wore when he celebrated Mass inside that prison camp.

As the sun rose that Easter Sunday, he put on that purple stole and led dozens of prisoners to the ruins of an old church in the camp. And he read from a prayer missal that they had kept hidden. He held up a small crucifix that he had made from sticks. And as the guards watched, Father Kapaun and all those prisoners — men of different faiths, perhaps some men of no faith — sang the Lord's Prayer and "America the Beautiful." They sang so loud that other prisoners across the camp not only heard them, they joined in, too — filling that valley with song and with prayer.

That faith — that they might be delivered from evil, that they could make it home — was perhaps the greatest gift to those men; that even amidst such hardship and despair, there could be hope; amid their misery in the temporal they could see those truths that are eternal; that even in such hell, there could be a touch of the divine. Looking back, one of them said that that is what "kept a lot of us alive."

Yet, for Father Kapaun, the horrific conditions took their toll. Thin, frail, he began to limp, with a blood clot in his leg. And then came dysentery, then pneumonia. That's when the guards saw their chance to finally rid themselves of this priest and the hope he inspired. They came for him. And over the protests and tears of the men who loved him, the guards sent him to a death house — a hellhole with no food or water — to be left to die.

And yet, even then, his faith held firm. "I'm going to where I've always wanted to go," he told his brothers. "And when I get up there, I'll say a prayer for all of you." And then, as was taken away, he did something remarkable —- he blessed the guards. "Forgive them," he said, "for they know not what they do." Two days later, in that house of death, Father Kapaun breathed his last breath. His body was taken away, his grave unmarked, his remains unrecovered to this day.

The war and the awful captivity would drag on for another two years, but these men held on — steeled by the memory and moral example of the man they called Father. And on their first day of freedom, in his honor, they carried that beautiful wooden crucifix with them.

Some of these men are here today — including Herb Miller, the soldier that Father Kapaun saved in that ditch and then carried all those miles. Many are now in their 80s, but make no mistake, they are among the strongest men that America has ever produced. And I would ask all of our courageous POWs from the Korean War to stand if they're able and accept the gratitude of a grateful nation.

I'm told that in their darkest hours in the camp in that valley, these men turned to a Psalm. As we prepare for the presentation of the Medal of Honor to Father Kapaun's nephew, Ray, I want to leave you with the words of that Psalm, which sustained these men all those years ago.

> Even though I walk in the valley of the shadow of death,
> I will fear no evil, for you are with me;

Your rod and your staff, they comfort me.
You prepare a table for me in the presence of my enemies.
You anoint my head with oil; my cup overflows.
Surely, your goodness and love will follow me all the days of my life.
And I will dwell in the house of the Lord forever.

Ray, would you please join me on stage for the reading of the citation?

Medal of Honor Citation

MILITARY AIDE: The President of the United States of America, authorized by Act of Congress, March 3, 1863, has awarded in the name of Congress the Medal of Honor to Chaplain Emil J. Kapaun, United States Army, for conspicuous gallantry and intrepidity at the risk of his life above and beyond the call of duty.

Chaplain Emil J. Kapaun distinguished himself by acts of gallantry and intrepidity above and beyond the call of duty while serving with the 3rd Battalion, 8th Cavalry Regiment, 1st Calvary Division during combat operations against an armed enemy at Unsan, Korea, from November 1st to 2nd, 1950.

On November 1st, as Chinese Communist Forces viciously attacked friendly elements, Chaplain Kapaun calmly walked through withering enemy fire in order to provide comfort and medical aid to his comrades and rescue friendly wounded from no-man's land.

Though the Americans successfully repelled the assault, they found themselves surrounded by the enemy. Facing annihilation, the able-bodied men were ordered to evacuate. However, Chaplain Kapaun, fully aware of his certain capture, elected to stay behind with the wounded.

After the enemy succeeded in breaking through the defense in the early morning hours of November 2nd, Chaplain Kapaun continually made rounds as hand-to-hand combat ensued. As Chinese Communist Forces approached the American position, Chaplain Kapaun noticed an injured Chinese officer amongst the wounded and convinced him to negotiate the safe surrender of the American forces.

Shortly after his capture, Chaplain Kapaun, with complete disregard for his personal safety and unwavering resolve, bravely pushed aside an enemy soldier preparing to execute Sergeant First Class Herbert A. Miller. Not only did Chaplain Kapaun's gallantry save the life of Sergeant Miller, but also his unparalleled courage and leadership inspired all those present, including those who might have otherwise fled in panic to remain and fight the enemy until captured.

Chaplain Kapaun's extraordinary heroism and selflessness above and beyond the call of duty are in keeping with the highest traditions of military service and reflect great credit upon himself, the 3rd Battalion, 8th Cavalry Regiment, the 1st Calvary Division, and the United States Army.

CHAPLAIN RUTHERFORD: And let us pray together:

Lord, God, let us go forth into the world in peace and dedication to your service. Let us follow Chaplain Kapaun's example and hold fast to that which is good; render to no person evil for evil; strengthen the faint-hearted. May we support the weary, encourage the tired, and honor all peoples. Let us love and serve, and may God's blessing be upon us, pray with us today and always, as we ask and pray in your Holy Name. Amen.

THE PRESIDENT: Well, I can't imagine a better example for all of us — whether in uniform or not in uniform, a better example to follow. Father Kapaun's life I think is a testimony to the human spirit, the power of faith, and reminds us of the good that we can do each and every day regardless of the most difficult of circumstances. We can always be an instrument of his will.

So, I hope all of you have enjoyed this ceremony. I certainly have been extremely touched by it. To the Kapaun family, God bless you. To all our veterans, we're so proud of you.

President Obama Awards Medal of Honor to Father Emil Kapaun

APRIL 11, 2013 AT 4:29 PM ET BY COLLEEN CURTIS
https://obamawhitehouse.archives.gov/blog/2013/04/11/president-obama-awards-medal-honor-father-emil-kapaun-0

Summary:

President Obama bestowed the nation's highest honor on a remarkable man who gave his life serving God and country in the Korean War. Read the story of his incredible bravery.

President Barack Obama embraces Ray Kapaun after presenting him with the Medal of Honor awarded posthumously to his uncle, Chaplain (Captain) Emil J. Kapaun, during a ceremony in the East Room of the White House, April 11, 2013. Chaplain Kapaun was awarded the medal for his extraordinary heroism while serving with the 3d Battalion, 8th Cavalry Regiment, 1st Cavalry Division during combat operations against an armed enemy at Unsan, Korea and as a prisoner of war from November 1-2, 1950. (Official White House Photo by Pete Souza)

Prologue

In steamy July 1950, the Korean War was a month old with deadly skirmishes breaking out in several areas simultaneously and civilian casualties already escalating. The energetic North Korean People's Army (KPA) invasion resulted in the near-collapse of the South Korean (Republic of Korea or ROK) forces. Pushed back into the Pusan Perimeter, south of the 38th parallel, the South Koreans relied on the swift and numerous reinforcements from the United Nations and, principally, the United States, to stabilize the situation.

Master Sergeant Bill Richardson of the 3rd Battalion, 8th Cavalry Regiment, 1st Cavalry Division, a tough no-nonsense leader on the battlefield, crawled like a toddler towards the forward edge of the front line. A tall, heavily built man, he was liked by all despite the fact that he always knew how things should be done and disagreed with anyone who didn't think the way he did, regardless of rank. He was right more often than not. He jumped as explosions rang out across the jumbled battlefield.

Several American soldiers cautiously trawled their way through the brush, guns at the ready, keeping low to the ground through the tall grass so as not to get their heads shot off. The area was already crammed with the bodies of dead soldiers from both sides. The bloody ground was swampy with littered human body parts; for the past few hours, this area had been fought over repeatedly with neither side able to win the field.

The master sergeant crawled past yet another dead American soldier, the air around him already filling with flies. He shook his head, devastated by the number of lives that had been lost in such a short time. He stopped and placed his hand over the man's eyes, closing them forever. To his left, two other American soldiers were lying on the ground, recently injured; one was bleeding profusely from the chest. Richardson winced. The worst wound possible. He made his way towards them to see if he could save the life of at least one person today.

As he crawled towards the bleeding soldiers, he saw something out of the corner of his eye and froze in place. It was a North Korean soldier. This one was walking briskly toward Richardson, seemingly unaware of his presence and unafraid of the consequences of walking upright through a battlefield.

Richardson carefully aimed his M1 Garand rifle at the man and shot him, putting two bullets into the soldier's throat; the man dropped his gun, grabbed his throat, and fell to the ground — Dead. Two other enemy soldiers began to run away as the master sergeant aimed his gun at one of them and tried to fire again; but before he could get another shot off, his rifle jammed. He slammed it on the ground in frustration.

Lieutenant Mike Dowe and Private First Class Tibor Rubin, bent over, ran toward the master sergeant, both standing briefly to fire their rifles, hitting the enemy soldiers in the head and chest, killing them before they could complete their escape. Dowe and Rubin immediately flopped to the ground.

Richardson sat up, pounded on his rifle, the anger welling up in him. So many lost, so little to be done. After a few moments, he calmed down and nodded at Dowe and Rubin. "Thanks, Mike, Tibor. Thought they had my ass there for a second."

"No problem, Bill," Dowe replied. He looked as relieved as the master sergeant. He was an easy-going small man with a great capacity for compassion.

"Just glad we were here," Rubin added. His thick Hungarian accent blended the words together, so they sounded like a chant.

Richardson looked around, alert, still annoyed as he finally managed to eject the stuck cartridge and cycled another into his rifle's chamber. He turned back to his companions. "How do they expect us to fight with these crappy ass weapons?"

"I don't know. Supplying us with better guns is a no-brainer if you ask me," Dowe responded.

"Exactly," Richardson replied. But even he knew his frustration was only partly with the rifle.

"Mine works fine," Rubin said, smiling.

Richardson and Dowe glanced at Rubin, then looked at each other, rolling their eyes.

Lieutenant Dowe was a tough career-soldier with loyalties to Master Sergeant Richardson and enjoyed the confidence of the rest of his platoon. He could always be counted on to have everyone's back. He seemed to take the responsibility easily.

Tibor Rubin, on the other hand, was often misunderstood, in part due to his heavy Hungarian accent and limited command of English. He had an eagle eye and was proud of his abilities, and often he came off as cocky. But he was a team player.

Captain William Shadish scuttled to the group, staying low to the ground, surveying the area.

"That all of 'em?" Shadish asked.

"As far as I can tell, Sir," Richardson replied, saluting Captain Shadish.

Shadish waved the salute away, looking to the left and right, behind him. Enemy snipers were his concern, not army protocol. He had a snappish temper and was only concerned with two things: winning this war and getting back home.

"Good. Let's —" The Captain was interrupted as enemy gunfire started up again. They all hit the ground as a stream of bullets flew low over their heads. Behind them, an American soldier stood and got one shot off before being riddled with bullets from two more enemy soldiers.

From about ten yards to the left, Corporal Walt Gray quickly fired, taking out both of the advancing enemy soldiers.

Shadish, still crawling, moved over to Gray, smiling and relieved.

"Way to make them pay, Gray," Shadish said.

"Always vigilant, Sir," Gray replied, keeping his eyes on the enemy-controlled area to his front.

Richardson looked at Dowe. "I was afraid he was gonna rhyme something back."

Dowe laughed. It echoed over the terrain, sounding out of place. He and the master sergeant looked over at the American soldier who'd just a few moments ago been shot and silently shook their heads.

"We've lost too many good men already. Makes me sick," Richardson said.

"We can't just leave him there. We don't even know if he's dead," Dowe replied.

"I don't know what to tell you. I'd say, 'war is hell,' but somebody already beat me to it," Richardson said glumly.

They all grunted at the master sergeant's comment, but then they saw something that took their breaths away. Their half-smiles turned into looks of confusion and awe as they watched a tall, slender man with protruding ears and a rosary in his hand walk upright across the field, headed towards the downed soldier.

Richardson looked over at Shadish in disbelief. "Captain, who's that?"

"Think it's our new chaplain, Father Kapaun," Shadish shouted.

"What the hell's wrong with that guy, walking like he doesn't have a care in the world?" Dowe asked. "Doesn't he know this is war?"

"All I know is, this is no place for a chaplain," Shadish replied, his brow furrowed.

Father Kapaun knelt and leaned over the fallen soldier to begin performing the sacrament of the sick. They saw him make the cross and touch the boy's mouth with the rosary. They couldn't hear the words he mouthed.

"Gotta hand it to him, he's the most fearless chaplain I've ever seen," Richardson commented.

"You can say that again," Rubin said, turning his head so he could watch the chaplain.

"Hopefully, he'll live long enough for that to mean something," Shadish said as he snorted.

"I have a feeling he'll be just fine," Gray added. He looked on approvingly.

Part One — Off to War

"The true soldier fights not because he hates what is in front of him, but because he loves what is behind him."

— G.K. Chesterton

"God created war so that Americans would learn geography."

— Mark Twain

Chapter 1

July 18, 1950
Korea Strait

F ather Kapaun stood near a porthole on the USS Mt. McKinley, looking out at the choppy gray water below. He was on his way from Japan to this unknown country of Korea, he said a small prayer of hope. What was it the girl in the movie had said? "We're not in Kansas anymore." Truer words were never spoken. He was on his way to Korea, a place he'd hardly heard about a few weeks before. He wasn't looking forward to it, but he had his orders from God and that meant everything to him. At the age of thirty-four, he'd fought in World War Two, where been stationed in Burma and seen some things he wouldn't want to tell his best friend about. He ran his hand through his short brown hair then reached into his pocket and brought out a pipe and a bag of tobacco. As he was lighting the pipe, he turned, feeling a presence.

He saw a tall, dark-haired woman standing nearby, watching him. She walked up to him.

"Hi, Father. I'm Sally."

"I'm Father Kapaun. Are you okay, Sally? You look a bit nervous." He reached out and put his hand on her arm. He noted her white complexion and darting eyes.

1

"I guess I am a little nervous. This trip has been a lot more to deal with than I expected. I don't understand the politics; I am just going to Korea to nurse the soldiers. I lost an older brother in the war a few years ago."

"No one but the generals understands why we're here, Sally," Father Kapaun said. "Did you lose your brother in World War Two?"

"Yes. I thought I'd do what I could to keep the soldiers safe. But sometimes my hands start shaking and I question every single decision I've made." She held her hands tight in front of her. Kapaun noticed her face tense up, she looked about to cry.

"I'm sorry to hear about your brother, Sally."

"Thank you, Father. I miss him. He teased me mercilessly, you know, as we were growing up, but I loved him."

"I know losing him must've been hard. I applaud you for your brave decision to come out and help. Most people would not do what you are doing."

Sally smiled wistfully. "That's very kind of you, Father."

"I hope you know that God is with us. Always. Whatever happens is God's will. You're a young woman and you seem like a good person. The thought of dying, when you have your whole life ahead of you, can certainly be scary."

"It scares me to death at times," Sally said, wrapping her arms around herself.

"Just remember, we are all only here for a short while, whether it's a hundred years or a hundred seconds. But Heaven is where you will spend eternity once God is ready for you and you'll never be frightened or unhappy there."

"Thank you, Father. That's not exactly what I was hoping to hear, yet I find it oddly comforting somehow." She leaned over and hugged him.

"I'm glad I could help, dear."

She smiled at Father Kapaun and walked away, pulling her shoulders back and wiping an errant tear from her eye.

Kapaun relit his pipe as he watched her walk away.

Standing not 20 feet away, Corporal Walt Gray also watched Nurse Sally, unable to take his eyes off her until she was no longer in sight. He walked over to Father Kapaun, smiling, his eyes bright.

"I'm Corporal Gray, but you can call me Walt, Sir." He held out his hand.

"Nice to meet you, Walt. I'm Father Kapaun." Kapaun shook Gray's offered hand.

"Can I ask you a question?" Gray asked.

"You just did," Father Kapaun replied.

They laughed.

"Okay, can I ask another one?" he said assertively.

"Fire away, son."

"What did you just say to Nurse Sally? I'd love to be able to put a smile on her face like that."

"Mostly we talked about her dying. It seemed to cheer her up."

Gray's eyes widened, his smile vanishing, he looked dumbfounded. "She's dying?"

Father Kapaun smiled at Gray and said, "We're all dying, but no, she's fine. You should go talk to her. She's very nice. I bet you could put a smile on each other's face."

Gray exhaled deeply; such was his relief. He thought a moment about Father Kapaun's advice. Nodding his head, he said, "Maybe I will. Thank you." As he turned and wandered away in the general direction Sally had headed.

Father Kapaun smiled and shook his head, saying quietly to himself, *Mom, you would've loved that one.* He smoked his pipe slowly, his mind now on his parents, and went back to looking out the porthole at the choppy water below. The water that already looked rougher than it had only moments ago. He found himself wondering if that was an ill omen. He'd seen a lot of death and destruction already during his ministry. But he didn't really believe in omens. There was only God's word.

Father Emil Kapaun's parents, Enos and Elizabeth "Bessie" Kapaun, sat outside on the front porch of their Kansas farm, gently rocking on the porch swing. The fields were a vibrant green and the earth was a rich brown. Enos's chores were done for the day and he was enjoying a glass of Bessie's homemade lemonade. The sky glowered a greenish-gray, threatening rain, but Bessie looked far more concerned than one should about the rain. Enos saw the worry written all over her face: her lovely blue eyes were scrunched up, her mouth was pressed firmly shut, and there were lines stretching across her forehead. He'd seen the same look years before when Emil was serving in South East Asia in the last war.

"What's wrong, Bessie?" Enos asked.

"Just thinking about Emil," Bessie replied shortly.

Enos nodded sympathetically and said, "I'm sure he's fine, honey. Remember, he came home from the last war in one piece. In fact, I think he came back a better person after being able to help so much. And I'm sure he's making a big difference over in Korea now as well. President Truman says we all need to fight Communism. I suppose we all need to try to make a difference."

"That's what I'm worried about. You can't make any kind of difference without sticking your neck out. And you know what happens to those who stick their necks out," she said, looking more worried by the second.

Enos sighed and noticed the wind had picked up. It was looking more and more like rain as the clouds thickened from the west.

"Don't you sigh at me. If I want to worry about our son, I will," Bessie said sternly.

"I didn't say 'not to worry.' I'm just saying God's watching over him. He'll be fine. He's a good boy," Enos said.

Bessie made a face at Enos and said, "I know he's a good boy. I just hate it when he's at war like this. Every second he's gone feels like an eternity. I miss him so much."

"I understand. I miss him, too. But I really believe he's going to be fine," Enos said, trying to comfort his beloved Bessie as best as he could.

"I hope you're right."

A thunderclap boomed and a bolt of lightning raced across the ever-darkening sky.

Bessie frowned and said, "And I hope that's not a sign."

"It's a sign I'd better shut things up, so the animals don't drown in their stalls. Be right back," Enos jumped up and ran off towards the barn.

Bessie looked up and spoke to God. "God, I know my husband's right, that you're watching over my son. And I'm sure he really is helping a lot of people. That's always been his way since he was a little boy. I just wish there was a way for me to know that he's all right. Like maybe putting an end to this crazy war so my boy could come home to his mama."

Suddenly, the rain came down hard and with the wind blowing like crazy, Bessie scooted inside the farmhouse, shaking her head woefully.

Early on the morning of July 18, 1950, the 8th Regiment of the 1st Cavalry Division successfully completed the first amphibious landing of the Korean War, near the South Korean town of Pohang-dong. Men and women, machinery, stores, and weapons surrounded them. Kapaun looked around, once again astonished to see the logistical operation it took to mount a war.

Captain Shadish signaled for everyone to gather around him. "Attention, I need to make an announcement."

Master Sergeant Richardson tapped Father Kapaun on the shoulder. "You should hear this, Father."

"Okay, thank you," Father Kapaun replied.

Richardson and Father Kapaun walked towards Captain Shadish along with a large group of over one hundred soldiers that included PFCs Tibor Rubin, Peter Busatti, Patrick Schuler, and Joe Ramirez, Corporal Walt Gray, Sergeants Herbert 'Pappy' Miller and Vincent Doyle, and Lieutenants Mike Dowe, Ralph Nardella, and Bob Wood.

Father Kapaun saw many familiar people, some of whom he'd spoken with on the ship; yet he also saw many new ones whom he felt excited to meet and help. He looked over at PFC Joe Ramirez whose hands were shaking so badly he had to put them behind his back. Joe glanced at Father Kapaun for a moment. He gave Father Kapaun a weak smile before turning his attention to Captain Shadish.

Shadish jumped up on a munitions box, cleared his throat, and raised his voice. "All right, gather round and listen up, soldiers. We have a lot we need to accomplish today. I have here a standing order from General Walker, which I'll read to you."

He pulled a piece of paper from his shirt pocket and cleared his throat again. The soldiers fidgeted, their attention split between the Captain and looking over the new terrain and one another. Captain Shadish began reading:

"We are fighting a battle against time. There will be no retreating. There will be no Dunkirk. There will be no Bataan. We must fight until the end; we must fight as a team to have any chance of succeeding. If some of us die, we will die fighting together. We will hold the line and we will win."

Shadish folded the paper and slipped it into his pocket. He looked the men and women over, many of whom would not make eye contact. "Is that clear to everyone? We are the first line against the evil that is Communism," Captain Shadish asked.

Everyone nodded. A few mumbled "Yes, Sir!" but the only emotion emanating from the troops was their fear. Kapaun could feel it; it was palpable. Saying there would be no retreating was like saying no second chances. You either kill everyone in front of you or die trying. That was a lot for everyone to digest, even the nurses who knew that order meant many full hospital beds and weeks of trying to save men.

Father Kapaun cleared his throat to get everyone's attention. Everyone looked at him. "Let us pray," he said.

Richardson bowed his head and everyone else followed suit except for Ramirez. After a moment, Joe realized he was the only one not bowing his head. He exhaled nervously and quickly bowed his head but didn't close his eyes. In his mind, he knew the enemy could be anywhere and a sniper could be aiming at him at that very moment. He brought his shaky hands together in front of him, locking his fingers tightly together.

Father Kapaun spoke, his voice sounding like it was coming from Heaven, "Glory be to the Father and to the Son and to the

Holy Spirit. As it was in the beginning, it is now, and ever shall be, a world without end. Amen."

Everyone said "Amen." As they lifted their heads, their spirits lifted as well. Kapaun's voice had stirred everyone. His words sounded angelic, as if they were from God himself. Everyone looked around at others standing nearby, and they smiled.

"Thank you, Father," Shadish said.

Father Kapaun smiled and nodded at the Captain. The tense moment was over, but only briefly. Just then a platoon of tanks began rolling off the ship and everyone was reminded where they were and what they were about to do. Communism or no, fear of the unknown clutched their bodies once again. Kapaun worked his way through the crowd shaking hands and touching a shoulder here and there.

Captain Shadish looked at his Master Sergeant and said, "Bill, I have something you're going to love."

Richardson looked surprised and confused. "Really?"

Captain Shadish threw open the flap of the supply tent with a flourish. The master sergeant stood outside the tent, his eyes wide, a big smile slowly creeping onto his face. Inside the tent were brand new M1 rifles, Browning Automatic Rifles, grenades, ammo, and several other items including rain gear, ponchos, and most importantly, socks.

"Are you serious, Captain?" Richardson asked, astounded.

"Have at it," Shadish replied, looking pleased with himself. These were the supplies the master sergeant had been asking the captain for when the battalion was still on its training grounds back in Japan, but which neither of them had thought they would ever get.

"If you were a girl, I'd kiss you right now," Richardson retorted, slapping Shadish on the back.

"See that you don't," Shadish replied, turned himself around, and walked off, pleased with himself. These new supplies could make a big difference to his company's morale, and they were going to need all the morale they could muster. The odds were stacked heavily against them. He'd heard that 75,000 North Korean soldiers had invaded the South. How were they to win a war when at such a numerical and material disadvantage?

Master Sergeant Richardson emitted a "Woo-hoo!" that was probably heard for miles around. It certainly brought the soldiers running. He turned and saw a throng of soldiers lining up behind him including Ramirez, Dowe, and Busatti.

"Line up, boys, let's get geared up!" Peter Busatti said.

Master Sergeant Richardson gathered two supply clerks who started taking names and coordinating the handout of supplies, under the watchful eyes of the lieutenants. Then he pulled weapons and supplies and meted them out for the soldiers in line.

Richardson was almost beside himself. He felt like Santa Claus doling out gifts to kids. He told those in line, "Everybody, check your gear. Remove any personal items from your bag. You need to make sure you have at least three pairs of socks in your bag. I don't want anyone dying of pneumonia in a pair of wet socks. Your whole life is about to depend on what you're carrying with you. Tomorrow morning, we'll be moving to an assembly area north of Taegu. Be ready to go." He added more solemnly, "You might want to take a minute to write home first since I don't know when you'll get your next chance."

Everyone nodded and moved forward, taking Master Sergeant Richardson's advice, taking several pairs of socks before even looking at the rifles and ammo.

A private at the back of the line yelled out, "All right! We're getting new guns!"

Master Sergeant Richardson stopped handing out gear and said in a loud, commanding voice, "Who said that? Did you call your weapon a 'gun'?"

Not wanting to get singled out, the private said in a meek voice, "I did, Sir!"

"Get up here, Private, now! First, I'm not a Sir, I'm a Master Sergeant, I work for a living. Second, Private, never, ever call a weapon a gun. A gun is an artillery piece, you're not in the artillery, you're in the infantry. Third, Private, don't you remember any of your Basic Training?"

"Uh...yes, Sir ... I mean Master Sergeant. "I remember ... but what part?"

"The part that goes like this," Richardson grabbed an M1, held it up in his right hand, grabbed his crotch with his left hand and shaking the raised M1 said, "This is my rifle!" He grabbed his crotch, "This is my gun!" Shaking the M-l he said, "This is for fighting!" Shaking his crotch, Richardson bellowed out, "This is for fun! You got that, Private?"

"Yes, Master Sergeant, I do remember our Drill Sergeant saying that." The private was shaking. "I've been thinking a lot more about fighting than having fun. Don't seem to be much of an opportunity for that around here. But sometimes, I think about that, too, Master Sergeant."

"Fight with one and guard the other, Private! I'd hate to see you going home without your family jewels ..." The other men gathered there let out oohs and aahs, wincing as they grabbed their groins.

☆ ☆ ☆

While the soldiers were kitting out, Father Kapaun walked into the battalion aid station tent and was pleasantly surprised to see only a few cots had been set up and were occupied. Although the 1st

Cavalry Division was still in the process of disembarking, other American units in the area had sent some of their wounded back to the beach at Pohang-dong, hoping they'd be evacuated back to Japan. The battalion's doctor, Doc Anderson, stood talking with a thick-set man, his short gray hair neat under a cap. The four nurses sat by themselves off to the side, talking. They smiled at Father Kapaun as he walked into the tent. Doc Anderson quietly spoke to the man before turning to Father Kapaun and nodding a greeting.

"Father Kapaun, have you met Chaplain Mills?" Doc Anderson asked.

Father Kapaun raised his eyebrows and said, "I can't say as I have. Chaplain?"

Chaplain Mills walked over to Father Kapaun, smiling, and extending his hand. The men shook hands.

"You've got quite a grip there, Father. I've heard many good things about you," Chaplain Mills said. "You're a real trooper."

"That's very kind of you. I try. Forgive my surprise, but I hadn't heard there was to be another chaplain in the camp."

"Oh, the army does what the army does. I guess they figured the number of soldiers warranted another one of us. I hope you're not upset. I'm sure there's enough work for the two of us."

"I hope people don't think having two chaplains here is too many," Father Kapaun said.

"The last thing I'm worried about is us stepping on each other's toes. In fact, once we get in the thick of battle, they may be saying two ain't enough," Chaplain Mills said. He took off his cap and rubbed his hand over his hair.

Father Kapaun laughed, "You might be right about that. It really is good to meet you. Nice to have another chaplain in the ranks. I think we're going to get along well."

"So do I," Chaplain Mills said, smiling broadly as he headed toward the tent's main door.

Nurse Deborah noticed Father Kapaun's presence and walked over to greet him. She was a slight, small woman whose sense of duty was nearly as strong as his own.

"Father Kapaun, it's nice to meet you. My father is a minister back in Texas," Deborah said.

"That's wonderful. It's always good to hear I'm not the only one," Father Kapaun said, chuckling.

Deborah allowed herself a giggle. "Can I help you with anything?"

"Could you tell me how the men are doing?" he inquired.

"They're not great. But they'll live. Let me introduce you to Lieutenant Martin. He's probably having the hardest time right now," she replied, her eyes suddenly serious and her manner professional.

She walked towards one of the beds as he followed her.

"Lieutenant Martin, this is Father Kapaun," Deborah said.

Martin glanced at Father Kapaun; his expression morose.

"Father?" Martin said.

Father Kapaun noticed that one of Martin's legs had been amputated and what remained of it was wrapped with several bandages. Lieutenant Martin had been serving with the 19th Infantry Regiment of the 24th Infantry Division and had been wounded in combat two days earlier.

"Son, I'm sure I don't have to tell you that this is an ugly war. Barely begun and already there have been many casualties. I'm sure you're happy to be leaving this place behind," Father Kapaun said.

"I'm not sure I'd say happy," Martin replied, frowning, looking down at what remained of his amputated leg.

Deborah looked down at her feet before looking back at Father Kapaun.

"I'll just leave you men to talk," Deborah said.

Father Kapaun nodded at her. She walked away.

Father Kapaun got closer to Martin and gave him a stern but compassionate look.

"Son, you have to be able to see the good in the bad, otherwise your life will be a lot harder than it needs to be. So, try to find happiness wherever you can," Father Kapaun advised.

Martin nodded, grimacing. A tear rolled down his cheek.

"I know you're right, Father. But I'm going home an invalid," he said.

Father Kapaun shook his head, looked deep into Lieutenant Martin's eyes, and said, "Better for you and your loved ones than going home in a body bag."

Martin nodded repeatedly, thinking it over. He wiped a tear away. "You're right. I don't know why I didn't see it like that."

"It's all right. It sometimes takes a while to wrap our heads around change. Let's pray," Father Kapaun said seeing that his words had an instant effect on Martin, began to pray as Martin, eyes closed, listened. The words soothed Martin in ways he had never expected.

Two beds away, Doc Anderson and Nurse Mary watched, transfixed, as Father Kapaun lifted Lieutenant Martin's spirits. They were deeply moved by what they saw.

"He knows just what to say to comfort them," Mary said.

Mary was a curious, intelligent woman who was not easy to impress.

"He comforts them by telling them the truth. Now that's a gift," Doc Anderson replied.

Doc Anderson had the ability to see right through someone and know exactly who they were the moment he met them, but he usually kept his insights to himself. But knowing that Mary was also very observant and insightful, he felt comfortable telling her his deepest thoughts, more so than anyone else in the camp.

Mary smiled. "You're right. It is," she said, nodding.

They watched as Father Kapaun finished praying with Martin.

Lieutenant Martin opened his eyes. He looked at Father Kapaun, moved, and said "Thank you, Father. I already feel better. I'll never forget you."

"Or me you, son. Be well." Father Kapaun said, laying a gentle hand on his shoulder. After a moment, Father Kapaun stood up. He saw Doc Anderson and Nurse Mary watching him and walked directly over to them.

"Hi, I'm Father Kapaun."

"I doubt there's a person in this whole company that doesn't already know who you are," Doc said vigorously shaking hands with Father Kapaun.

"I'm Doc Anderson and this is my head nurse, Mary. We overheard your conversation with Lieutenant Martin, and I have to say I was very impressed."

"So was I," Mary added.

"Thank you and it's nice to meet you both," Father Kapaun said.

"It's our pleasure, Father."

"You really lifted Lieutenant Martin's spirits. Thank you for that. He really needed it," Mary said gratefully.

"That's what I'm here for, Mary." Father Kapaun bent slightly at the waist; then he walked out of the tent.

☆ ☆ ☆

Father Kapaun left the battalion aid station tent, lit his pipe, and came face to face with Joe Ramirez.

"Father, may I have a word with you?" Joe asked.

"Of course. What's troubling you, son?" Father Kapaun replied. He took his pipe out of his mouth and tapped it on his shoe.

"First, I wanted to give you these," Joe said. Father Kapaun held his hands out and Joe put several pairs of socks into them. Kapaun looked confused.

"Sergeant Richardson said they could save your life," Joe said encouragingly.

Father Kapaun nodded and said, "I know how necessary it is to have dry feet. Thank you ..."

"Ramirez. Joe Ramirez."

"Thank you, Joe. Something else you wanted to talk about?" Kapaun knew the socks were only an excuse.

Joe sighed. He twisted his hands and then hid them behind his back. Finally, he said, "Just that I'm scared. I don't want to die out here, forsaken by God."

Father Kapaun looked him over with compassion. Joe felt slightly embarrassed for a moment. He twisted his hands again.

"Joe, God would never forsake you."

Joe nodded but did not look convinced. "I figured you'd say that."

Father Kapaun saw the doubt in Joe's eyes. He thought for a couple of seconds and then asked, "Have you been baptized, son?"

Joe shook his head.

"You know, it's never too late. God would never forsake you and baptism will help you feel His love."

Joe's face lit up. "Really?"

Father Kapaun smiled at Joe, knowing he was on the right track.

A few hours later, as the sun hung low in the sky, Father Kapaun stood on the beach with Joe Ramirez, preparing to baptize him. A majority of the troops stood nearby watching. Many were silent, their hands clasped in front of them. Some were praying. Some were smoking and talking quietly amongst themselves. Standing next to Father Kapaun was Chaplain Mills, preparing to baptize Eva.

Sergeant Richardson smiled at Deborah as they watched the events taking place. It was the largest baptism most of them had ever witnessed.

Standing next to Bill and Deborah were Sally and Walt hand in hand, both looking peaceful and happy.

Father Kapaun cleared his throat and said quietly but firmly, "We'll begin." The troops quieted down. He waded into the waves, Joe at his side.

He filled his helmet with the cold ocean water, roiled gray and green, and poured it over Joe's head as he said, "I baptize you in the name of the Father, and of the Son, and of the Holy Spirit."

Joe looked down at his hands. He was cold, but his hands had stopped shaking. He smiled.

Chaplain Mills, standing in the water, filled his helmet with water and poured it over Eva's head, saying "I baptize you in the name of the Father, and of the Son, and of the Holy Spirit." Eva began to cry quietly. Deborah ran to her and embraced her.

Several soldiers stood in line, each waiting patiently for their turn. Father Kapaun and Chaplain Mills continued this act of obedience as one person after another was baptized until the darkness descended. Suddenly, their words were drowned out by nearby ships unloading thousands of men and vehicles.

The next day, just before boarding the troop trains with the men gathered around, Captain Shadish looked over to Father Kapaun and said, "I have a sound system prepared to give final instructions to the men. Would you like to say something to them before we load up? I don't know how many people you baptized yesterday, Father, but I think you lifted a lot of spirits."

Eva smiled and said, "You can say that again. I feel better already."

Nurse Deborah put a hand on Eva's shoulder, smiling at her, and said, "Good for you to be a part of it. It was really special to watch."

Eva beamed. Shadish handed a microphone to Father Kapaun and said "With all the death and destruction we're about to see, I thought you could say a few words to everyone. You have a way of lifting the men's spirits."

"Not just the men's," Deborah said.

The nurses all smiled.

"Correction. Everyone's spirits," Shadish said.

Father Kapaun smiled, took the microphone, and said, "I'd be happy to, Captain."

Kapaun carefully got to his feet and took a breath. He looked around, checking out the people as well as the surrounding area as he considered what to say. Then he smiled and spoke loudly to the troops, "In the early ages of the Church, the officials of the Roman Empire gave the Christians a choice: either give up their Christian faith or be put to death. Never give up your faith! Stay the course, run the good race, finish the race even in the face of danger and receive your just rewards in heaven …"

Father Kapaun continued. "The Christian martyrs would not give up their faith and suffered death although they were innocent of any crime. Fear not, you are warriors!"

"Now history has repeated itself with the recent events in Korea. We must again make a choice between being loyal to our faith or giving allegiance to something which is not in alignment with our faith," Father Kapaun continued. He adjusted his footing.

"O God, we ask of Thee to give us the courage to be ever faithful to Thee. Blessed are those who are persecuted for righteousness' sake, for theirs is the kingdom of heaven."

PFC Peter Busatti, Lieutenant Ralph Nardella, and Lieutenant Bob Wood looked down at their hands, moved by Kapaun's words but unwilling to show it. They were soldiers after all. Yet a tear slid down Peter's cheek. All four nurses shed tears. Gray could not take his eyes off Sally. He wanted to embrace her, but here was not the place. Doc Anderson and Chaplain Mills nodded and smiled at one another as they watched Father Kapaun finish.

"But the peace God gives us is a gift which exists, in suffering, in want, even in time of war. Blessed are the peacemakers, for they will be called children of God."

Father Kapaun finished, carefully lowered himself down from the train, and handed the mic back to Captain Shadish. Shadish got to his feet and opened his mouth as if to speak, a tear falling down his cheek, but even he was too choked up to respond to the chaplain's words. Instead, he nodded at Father Kapaun, turned away looking toward the front of the train, and dried his eyes.

Chapter 2

July 19, 1950

Advancing towards Taegu

H undreds of U.S. soldiers were piled on top of flat railcars as the train raced toward Taegu, South Korea, where the division was to assemble and prepare before moving into battle with the North Koreans. A steady rain poured on them, but most were lucky enough to be wearing their new ponchos over their uniforms. Trash and the debris of war were strewn all around the villages that lined the tracks: old disabled weapons, discarded machinery. The villages looked bleak and gray in the steamy rain.

Captain Shadish sat up front in the train with Doc Anderson, the nurses, Corporal Walt Gray, Father Kapaun, and Chaplain Mills. Shadish looked around as they passed a small town. A few huts remained, burned out and barely standing. No animals or chickens were heard. He shuddered.

Sergeant Bill Richardson sat next to Lieutenant Mike Dowe.

"I bet everyone's going to be happy you told them to bring a lot of socks," Dowe said to Richardson.

"If they even listened," Richardson replied, looking doubtful.

"Oh, I listened. In fact, I went back for more this morning in case four pairs weren't enough, and they were all gone. Grabbed a couple more grenades though."

They laughed. But their laughter was short-lived.

As the train crossed a bridge, they noticed a small clearing where a half-dozen young Korean boys were standing guard with what appeared to be rifles. Dowe immediately reached for his weapon, but Richardson grabbed his hand, shaking his head at the young lieutenant. Dowe looked closer at the rifles and realized they were non-functional wooden toys. He exhaled, and nodded at his seasoned sergeant, thankful he hadn't shot a boy who was holding a toy gun. War really was hell.

They passed another village. The huts were burned out, but people were still living in them. A few chickens ran around. The feeling was one of desperation, gloom, and doom where there was little hope.

PFC Tibor Rubin and Sergeant Pappy Miller watched in horror, mouths wide open, as they passed dead women and children on the side of the road as the train rattled along.

The train slowed and came to a complete stop at an overcrowded train station. There was a mass of Korean refugees and enemy soldiers, many old and wounded, standing around in dirty, threadbare uniforms which hung off their bony frames. Their eyes were dark, almost dead looking. PFC Tibor Rubin and Sergeant Pappy Miller looked at each other. The nurses looked concerned as if they would climb down and help the injured right then and there. Kapaun, too, felt compassion for the men. No one asked for war. No one in it truly benefitted from it. There are no winners in war.

"You think they came from where we're going?" Miller asked. He was so appalled he couldn't look away.

"God, I hope not," Tibor responded.

Behind them, several large trucks and Jeeps drove up. Shadish stood and announced, "Okay, here's our ride."

Everyone stood and nervously began to exit the train, not knowing what their next destination held. In the moment they were grateful to be alive and afraid of the future.

☆ ☆ ☆

Captain William Shadish rode in the passenger seat of the lead Jeep of the 1st Calvary Division convoy, with a wet-behind-the-ears GI as his driver. Father Kapaun and Chaplain Mills sat in the back seat, looking out at the desolated landscape as a slew of Jeeps followed them along with several large troop-filled trucks bringing up the rear.

They drove slowly through the streets of Taegu heading north to their assembly area. North Korean infiltrators had been active in the city aiming to cause chaos behind the South Korean positions. The Americans passed abandoned burned-out tanks, Jeeps, trucks, and cannons. Ahead, an American Jeep, riddled with bullets, had crashed into a pole. Four American soldiers sprawled motionless in another Jeep; their heads had been cut off. A bloody ax lay on the ground next to the crashed Jeep. MPs and medics attended to the dead soldiers as they assessed the macabre scene. Civilians lined the streets, busily handing out apples, wine, and flowers.

"Unbelievable," Chaplain Mills said, shaking his head and looking as if he'd been hurt himself. Both Father Kapaun and Chaplain Mills gave the sign of the cross and blessed the dead as they drove by.

"Eternal rest grant unto them, O Lord. And let perpetual light shine upon them," Father Kapaun said. Even in Burma, he'd not seen such cruelty and destruction.

Shadish turned around to look at Kapaun. He simply shook his head. Kapaun rubbed his eyes, as the column rolled on, leaving the city behind, and entering the countryside beyond.

As they approached their destination, the captain's driver stopped the Jeep suddenly. Everyone could hear the Jeeps and trucks behind them slamming on their brakes.

"Soldier, why are you stopping?" Captain Shadish screamed at the driver.

The driver pointed ahead, speechless, his mouth open and his eyes wide. Captain Shadish looked ahead, and his jaw dropped.

Ahead of them, a few hundred yards distant, a platoon of five enemy T-34/85 tanks drove directly towards the convoy and they weren't slowing down.

"Captain, should we retreat?" the driver asked.

Captain Shadish looked for another moment, wanting to tell the driver to get them the hell out of there. Then he shook his head.

"There will be no retreat. We have our orders," Shadish responded. He quickly stood in the Jeep, turned, and addressed the men, yelling, "Prepare for battle!"

Captain Shadish and the driver jumped from the Jeep. Father Kapaun and Chaplain Mills jumped, too, and ran off in different directions; Father Kapaun to the left and Chaplain Mills to his right.

Following suit, everyone jumped from their vehicles and ran off, scattering everywhere. The four men of the Company Headquarters' bazooka team jumped from one of the trucks and quickly took up positions on either side of the road preparing to fire on the approaching enemy.

The tanks continued to roll towards them. At a distance of about 100 yards, the tanks stopped for a few seconds for the lead tank to fire on the lead Jeep, blowing it up only seconds after the men had exited. Chaplain Mills, being the last to exit the Jeep, was knocked down by the blast, stood up, blessed himself, and then began running again, looking for a place to take cover.

As the tanks came into range, the first bazooka team fired on the lead tank. The bazooka round bounced off the tank's armor with a deafening clang. As the second bazooka team got ready to fire, several American soldiers, as well as scores of local civilians who had been working at the side of the road, ran into a nearby field, scattering left and right. Kapaun watched in terror as mines exploded all over the field, killing soldiers and civilians alike, their heads and limbs blown off as if they had never been attached.

Enemy soldiers jumped off the backs of their tanks, shooting at anyone they could see. One saw Father Kapaun standing off to the side and shot at him, blowing his helmet off.

Father Kapaun quickly looked around. He saw a nearby foxhole and dove, headfirst, into it.

In the foxhole, Father Kapaun came face to face with Sergeant Vincent Doyle. Doyle's eyes widened when he saw Father Kapaun.

"Where's your helmet, Father?" Doyle asked.

"Seems I lost it, son," Father Kapaun responded.

"Not a good thing to lose, Father."

"I suppose not. Better than losing my head, though."

Vincent Doyle nodded.

Bullets slammed all around the foxhole. The men lowered their heads, trying to get away from the constant gunfire.

Sergeant Richardson stood anxiously with Lieutenant Wood behind a tree on the edge of the battlefield setting up an M2 60-mm light mortar. They had been able to grab only one bag of eight mortar bombs when they pulled the mortar out of their now incinerated Jeep.

"How do we take out one of those tanks?" Wood exclaimed. "They look unstoppable!"

"Nothing's unstoppable, Bob," Richardson replied.

Just then, they heard the sound of powerful engines coming from above and behind them. They looked up as a flight of three F-51 Mustang[1] fighter planes swooped down from the sky and dropped their bombs along the road, ping, ping, ping, taking out the first North Korean tank with a huge boom. They also hit several of the U.S. Jeeps at the front of the now-abandoned convoy, throwing one high in the air with it crashing down a flaming heap of scrap metal.

"Guess you're right, Bill," Wood said.

Enemy artillery shells and mortar rounds exploded all around the American positions. The noise was deafening. Two GIs dove into another foxhole close by. Shells hit the ground around and inside the foxhole, leaving only a smoldering crater. Kapaun risked raising his unhelmeted head to see what had happened in the other foxhole. He could tell the soldiers were dead. He quickly ducked back down.

A North Korean machine gunner opened fire, streaming red tracer rounds, cutting several American soldiers in half. Tibor Rubin and Dowe jumped from their foxhole and shot at the machine gunner repeatedly. The machine gunner fell, bleeding from so many places he was dead before he even hit the ground.

An enemy tank, its engine smoking from a bazooka hit, came to a stop. The tank's driver opened the hatch, popped up, and began shooting his submachine gun.

Richardson looked Wood in the eye and said, "Okay, this is your chance. You need to bring that down on him at just the right angle."

Lieutenant Wood nodded and picked up a mortar round, removed the four boosting charges from its tailfins, adjusted the mortar's sight for its minimum range of 200 yards, and fired at the

---

[1] The famous P-51 Mustang was redesignated the F-51 in 1948.

tank. The enemy tank driver had emptied the magazine of his submachine gun and was in the process of attaching another. Hearing a whistling sound, he looked up and saw the mortar shell coming and ducked, but it was already too late. The mortar shell landed inside the tank and the tank's ammunition exploded, lifting the turret clean off the tank and dropping it upside down behind the tank.

"Way to go! Great shooting!" Richardson said.

"Thank you! Woo-hoo!"

Behind the burned-out tank, there were the three remaining tanks along with only half a dozen or so enemy infantrymen. After seeing the second tank explode, they turned tail and headed at full speed toward the north.

Father Kapaun and Doyle climbed from their foxhole and smiled broadly as they watched the enemy retreat. Doyle jumped up and down, watching the enemy go.

"You better run!" he screamed in a taunting voice.

Father Kapaun said a little prayer, thanking God.

Rubin and Dowe climbed from a nearby foxhole, hardly the worse for wear, and watched along with Father Kapaun and Doyle.

"They'll be back. Probably at night when we're not expecting them. Not sure I'll sleep tonight," Rubin said in resignation.

"I hear that," Dowe said, hanging his head and walking off; Doyle followed him.

Kapaun took an apple out of his pocket and offered it to Rubin.

Tibor looked shocked by the act of kindness.

"Fresh fruit? Thank you, Father," Rubin said, taking the apple and biting into it.

"You're welcome."

"By the way, I'm Tibor Rubin. From Hungary."

Rubin held the apple up like it was a present from God. Looking at Father Kapaun he added, "This is a real mitzvah, as my mother would say."

"Mitzvah?" Father Kapaun asked.

"Yes. It's Yiddish for 'good deed.' When you give out mitzvahs, mitzvahs come back to you. My mother told me when you save someone's life, you might be saving an entire nation. You never know."

"Your mother sounds like a smart woman."

"Oh, she is."

Rubin smiled for a moment, then began chomping down on the apple again.

Father Kapaun smiled at Rubin, then walked off towards Doc Anderson and Nurse Mary who knelt by a soldier who'd been shot, his eyes closing. Doc Anderson looked up at Father Kapaun. "He's not going to make it, Father." Father Kapaun knelt and began giving the soldier last rites. "Through this holy anointing, may the Lord in his love and mercy help you with the grace of the Holy Spirit. May the Lord who frees you from sin save you and raise you up."

☆ ☆ ☆

The sun finally went down on that gruesome day. Captain Shadish had evaluated the situation with the decreased number of vehicles and took into consideration the possibility that the enemy would return. He ordered the establishment of a perimeter and the posting of lookouts. The aid station was set up near his command post and the wounded were taken there for care. During a radio call with the regiment's commanding officer, he learned that the assembly area ahead of them was still under US control and that they were to move there the following morning. The enemy force they had run into was suspected of being a reinforced reconnaissance company that had slipped through a gap in the front lines, current whereabouts unknown.

Several American soldiers sat around fires. Many slept, as best they could. Some wrote letters home. Father Kapaun sat outside the aid station and wrote to his bishop who would be wondering how he and God's message were doing in Korea.

"Dear Bishop Carroll,

I hope this letter finds you well and in God's grace. I am well. God keeps me going even when things get tough. I have seen more death and destruction in this past day than I had seen in a month in Burma. I don't know what it is about people needing to kill, maim, hurt one another, but of course, war brings out the worst in them.

I minister to the men and women in my camp of course. Recently, the other chaplain and I baptized several dozen of the troops. This seemed to raise their spirits significantly. I thank God for His suggestion.

Ministering to the troops keeps my spirits up as well. We go through such horrors and I try to remind the men and women here that God is always present, helping us, loving us. I do wonder, sometimes, how they and I go on when I walk into the camp hospital and see dozens of young men torn apart, some dying, all suffering.

You may have heard the rumor that more than ten thousand Koreans—from both North and South—died in skirmishes at the border before we even arrived in S. Korea. I know we're fighting against the godless Communism, but it is hard to believe so many are willing to die for it.

I miss Kansas and my parents' farm, but I will persevere with God's help.

Your brother in God's Grace,

Emil Kapaun."

He put his head down and swiftly fell into a deep sleep.

Other soldiers sat together in small groups, trying to comfort one another, grateful they had made it through the day. The guards were further forwards, nowhere to be seen.

A North Korean soldier snuck into the camp. He saw a GI in a foxhole sound asleep and looked around, making sure no one had noticed him. Using the bayonet on the end of his rifle, he stabbed the sleeping man in the throat multiple times, killing the soldier. He smiled as he looked down at the dead GI, his throat slit, pleased with himself for killing the man without making a sound.

Sergeant Pappy Miller seated on the ground some twenty yards away turned abruptly and saw the North Korean soldier standing over the dead GI. Miller grabbed his rifle and shot the North Korean multiple times in the head and neck, waking everyone who had managed to fall asleep. Everyone in the immediate vicinity looked around and saw the dead North Korean soldier lying on the ground next to the dead GI. It didn't look like anyone else would fall asleep again that night.

Corporal Walt Gray and Nurse Sally rose from a foxhole they were getting cozy in. He looked around carefully. He saw another enemy soldier had slipped by the sentries and into the camp. He grabbed his gun and shot the enemy soldier in the back of the head. All the while, Sally watched Walt while keeping herself low inside the foxhole. He turned and looked at her, and lowered himself back into the foxhole.

Suddenly, they heard bugles and saw red and green flares bursting in the night sky. Hundreds of enemy soldiers charged their position.

Father Kapaun woke to screams and gunfire. He looked all around. Then he rose quickly and found cover, so he could get his bearings before moving forward toward the perimeter.

Joe Ramirez shot one of the first onrushing enemy soldiers. Sergeant Richardson and Lieutenant Dowe, twenty feet apart, stood and took out several soldiers each at a distance before they could get close enough to do any damage. Many of the American soldiers who were sleeping seconds earlier were now shooting at anything that moved.

Captain Shadish ran out of the command post and saw a pair of infiltrators headed towards him carrying what looked like satchel charges. He fired once and shot an enemy soldier with a round that not only took down that soldier but passed straight through him, taking out the second enemy soldier immediately behind him.

An enemy soldier entered the aid station and rushed towards Nurse Mary, a big smile on his face. She turned, grabbed a scalpel, dodged her attacker before turning around and slicing his neck open. Blood poured from his neck as she followed up her attack with a kick that put him on the ground. She looked down at herself. Her uniform was covered in blood and it made her feel horrific fear. This wasn't the blood of the soldiers she worked on in the operating room. This felt different, it was the blood of the enemy trying to take her own life.

PFC Rubin, who had been posted as a lookout, lobbed several grenades down the slope to his front, killing dozens of enemy soldiers. A mortar round exploded near Rubin, knocking him to the ground, unconscious.

Father Kapaun saw Rubin fall to the ground and ran to him, kneeling by his side and yelling, "Medic! We need a medic over here!"

Father Kapaun began praying by Rubin's side, saying, "Through this holy anointing may the Lord in his love and mercy

31

help you with the grace of the Holy Spirit. May the Lord who frees you from sin, save you and raise you up."

Rubin's eyes opened. He sat up and coughed. He looked at Kapaun.

"Father, you know I'm Jewish, right?" Rubin said.

"I don't know any Jewish prayers, son," Father Kapaun admitted.

"That's okay. I think I'm dying so any prayer should do."

"You're not dying as long as I'm here, Tibor."

Rubin smiled and said, "Boy, you're giving out lots of mitzvahs today!"

Rubin's eyes rolled up in his head and he lost consciousness again. A medic reached the scene along with Nurse Eva and they attended to Rubin. Father Kapaun said another prayer and then carefully stood and looked at the chaos around him.

He soon ducked and crawled his way toward other fallen soldiers. Shots seemed to be coming from all sides. It was hard to see who was where because of the smoke and dust. Kapaun saw PFC Patrick Schuler stab an enemy soldier with his bayonet, PFC Peter Busatti shot another enemy soldier through the eye, and Lieutenant Ralph Nardella ripped a rifle from an enemy soldier's hands, turn it around, stabbed him, then used the rifle to shoot several more enemy soldiers. Kapaun saw an injured GI on the ground and ran to him. The man had been shot in the head, and Father Kapaun knew he was not going to make it. He knelt down and looked at the man, barely alive.

"May the Lord Jesus protect you and lead you to eternal life," Father Kapaun said, bullets whizzing by him as explosions rocked the entire area, but none of it was more important at the moment than giving this dying man a last prayer.

Once the fighting abated and it was clear the enemy had been soundly beaten, Father Kapaun returned to the camp's rear and entered the aid station. There he provided comfort to the injured and dying, assisting Doc Anderson with the flow of casualties.

☆ ☆ ☆

The next day, Father Kapaun stood inside a tent overflowing with rows of stretchers, each containing a dead American soldier covered by a rain poncho. The stench was intense. Battalion HQ personnel attended to the identification process, under the supervision of Captain Shadish. Father Kapaun, handkerchief over his nose, stopped at each stretcher to say a prayer for the dead over the soldier before moving on to the next one. Nearby, Chaplain Mills did the same. Kapaun wondered how many they'd lost, but he didn't want to ask; he knew better than to count, it was too upsetting.

Many people gathered just outside the tent, silent and grieving over the previous day's losses. Some of them had tears in their eyes; others were angry and frowning. It was all such a nightmare.

"What are they doing with their bodies?" Walt asked.

"Hopefully getting them home to their families. Right, Doc?" Nurse Sally replied.

"I hope so. But we're at war. They'll do the best they can," Doc answered.

"You're not sure they'll get them home?" Nurse Mary asked, her face a mask of concern and fear. What if she were to die and they couldn't get her home? A vision of her parents and her younger brother came to her. They were standing over an empty grave. She shivered.

Doc Anderson scrunched his face up but did not answer. He'd seen this catastrophe before. He knew that sometimes it was hard to get all the dead home despite the Army's policy of doing just that.

"Let's take these bastards down and make sure there aren't any more casualties on our side," Lieutenant Dowe said, furious at the mounting losses. And yet he knew his fury was directed at the whole situation, not just the idea that they'd lost so many men. Why were they here at all in what seemed like a God-forsaken land fighting Communists so the world would stay safe? He didn't know if he even believed that line anymore. He kept his mouth shut.

"Well said, Lieutenant," Sergeant Richardson added, nodding his head.

☆ ☆ ☆

An hour later, the 1st Calvary convoy was moving forward deeper into South Korea once more, although now with fewer vehicles than before. Besides those lost in the ambush, a small column of vehicles carrying the dead and wounded headed back to the relative safety of Taegu. As a result, the advancing soldiers found themselves and their equipment crammed together. Sergeant Richardson rode in Captain Shadish's Jeep along with the two chaplains and an increasingly nervous driver. The convey moved more cautiously than the day before and it seemed an eternity before it arrived at the 1st Cavalry's designated assembly area near the city of Waegwan.

Shadish placed Richardson in charge of setting up the command post as he left to attend a meeting with Major General Hobart R. Gay the division's commanding officer. Father Kapaun helped Doc Anderson organize the aid station along with the four nurses, Corporal Gray and Sergeants Miller and Doyle. PFC Rubin feeling almost 100% again carried in equipment boxes. When they were finished Father Kapaun stepped outside and lit his trusty pipe. Nurse Deborah soon joined him.

"Father Kapaun. I heard you were very brave yesterday," she said, smiling and making a slight, respectful curtsy.

"Thank you, Deborah. That's very kind of you to say," Father Kapaun replied, overcome by a wave of embarrassment. To himself, he was only behaving as he always had and did not expect anyone to thank him for it, especially not in the middle of a war like this, a war that was tearing apart a country and so many people.

The 8th Cavalry Regiment was soon assigned and took up positions along the east side of the Naktong River and for a few days, it seemed that the military situation was stabilizing. Father Kapaun tended to the men's spiritual needs always appearing wherever any enemy attacks occurred.

Corporal Walt Gray had not forgotten Nurse Sally. He kept finding her and talking with her until he thought she was susceptible. Tall and muscular, Gray stood 5'11" in his stocking feet. His auburn hair was, as per Army regs, short and slick, but Sally could tell it was lush in its civilian life.

Sally James was tall, too. She'd always been the tall one in the family. Her father said she got it from her grandfather who had stood over six feet tall. Her long brown hair was usually up in a twist.

Walt had followed Sally on the ship that brought them to Korea, asking her about dying and why she was thinking about it. She discovered that he'd been talking to the Father. She lightly played it down and they talked about their hometowns. Since then, they'd been as inseparable as the Army would allow.

"Why don't you let me take you out?" Walt said one day.

"Take me out? Where? We're in the middle of a war," Sally replied, spreading her arms wide.

"Oh, I've got an idea," he said mysteriously.

"Okay. I'm interested." She smiled warmly. Walt was the kind of guy she'd been trying to meet in the States. Just because they were in a war didn't mean she was going to walk away from him.

The next day, he came to the nurses' tent with a big basket on his arm and a blanket thrown over his shoulder. He was dressed in his uniform, but it was impeccably clean and pressed.

"I've come to take you on a picnic," he said.

Sally laughed. "A picnic? In this heat, in this country?"

"Yep."

"Okay." She put her arm through his and they walked off.

Walt took her to a grove of trees up on a small hill not too far from camp. He'd scouted for days before asking Sally. Here they could relax, still see the camp, and be safe from enemy fire.

He grandly spread out the blanket and offered his hand to Sally. She took advantage of his assistance to sit gracefully on the blanket, drawing her knees underneath her and tucking her skirt in.

Then Walt sat down with the basket between his knees and began to unpack the goodies he'd spent some time and money to acquire.

"So, for madam's pleasure, we have the ever-popular Spam, some dubious cheese nuggets, bread which was baked during the second world war, and chef's famous dessert, banana pudding."

Sally giggled. "How did you manage to get all this stuff?"

"Oh, a little arm-bending here, a coin or two there. You know, the Army way."

"But the pièce de résistance is this," he said as he flourished a bottle of wine.

"Good heavens, Walt," Sally said. "That's a major acquisition. That's more than arm-bending and a few coins."

Walt smiled so hard, he blushed. "Yes, well, we have our ways."

Time went by as they ate and talked so that when Walt looked up, he realized the sun was deep in the western sky. He needed to get them back to camp.

"I had a nice time, Walt," said Sally. "You really went all out."

"Sally, there's something I need to say." He hesitated. "I'd do it again. In a heartbeat. I really like you." He blushed again.

"Walt, thank you. I like you, too. Though I'm not very good at arm-bending…"

"No need. That's what you've got me for," he said shyly.

Chapter 3

August 18, 1950

The Bowling Alley

In the second week of August, reports were received that the North Koreans were concentrating forces to the north of Taegu and the Republic of Korea (South Korea) 1st Infantry Division's sector. General Walker requested that any men that could be spared should be sent to meet this threat …

PFC Patrick Schuler drove a Jeep with a trailer attached near the rear of the 3rd Battalion convoy. Chaplain Mills sat shotgun in the front seat; Father Kapaun and Lieutenant Ralph Nardella rode in the back.

"This is so beautiful," Chaplain Mills said, looking all around, taking in the landscape. Hot though it was, the land was fertile and where the war had not touched it, quite scenic.

"It's called the bowling alley," Schuler said.

"Wish I'd brought my bowling shoes," Chaplain Mills said.

Everyone laughed, with Chaplain Mills laughing the loudest.

"Why do they call it the bowling alley?" Nardella asked.

"It has something to do with the sound effects coming from the valley," Schuler responded.

"What sounds?" Nardella asked, looking confused.

"Just listen," Father Kapaun said.

Everyone was silent, but the convoy's noise may it hard to hear anything from the surrounding countryside. Some odd sounds reverberated through the valley and they all became apprehensive. They looked around.

Straight ahead, they saw a thirty-foot-high stone wall with an ancient Buddhist temple behind it as they entered the village of Soi-ri. Here, too, the war had done its damage. Bombed out huts, trash, dead bodies: all were scattered throughout the village.

Refugees walked past. They looked warily at the Americans in the convoy. An old Papa-San sat with two small boys next to a bombed-out hut. The Papa-San looked up, saw them, and made the sign of the cross. Father Kapaun noticed, smiled, and said, "Patrick, let's stop here for a minute."

"We need to stay with the convoy, Father," Schuler said.

"Patrick, let Father Kapaun bless these people. Besides, I need to take a leak. We'll be back on the road in less than two minutes," Chaplain Mills said.

"All right, but two minutes tops," Schuler responded.

PFC Schuler pulled over to the side of the road and stopped, looking uncomfortable. He watched as Chaplain Mills ran behind a burned-up hut. He saw Father Kapaun and Lieutenant Nardella walk over towards the Papa-San. Father Kapaun held a can of Spam, his rosary, candy, and some C-rations in his hand.

A Jeep drove by with Corporal Gray in the passenger seat. Gray held his hands up in a questioning gesture to PFC Schuler as if asking why they had stopped. Schuler gave Gray a thumbs up. Corporal Gray nodded and turned back around in his seat. The rest of the convoy passed by without question and disappeared around the bend. Schuler could hear it long after it had gone by. He shifted in his seat.

Father Kapaun handed out food and candy. Everyone looked thrilled: the children stuffed candy in their mouths, and the Papa-San accepted the C-rations, looking grateful. Kapaun began to pray with the old man, the rosary sifting through his fingers.

Suddenly a loud crashing noise, like a hundred bowling pins being knocked over, got everyone's attention.

The villagers scattered in an instant. Father Kapaun's eyes widened as he looked at Lieutenant Nardella, his mouth twisted into a question. "Where's the Chaplain?" he yelled.

Nardella shook his head. "I'll find him! Get to the Jeep, Father!"

Father Kapaun nodded and ran toward the Jeep, looking around. A mortar round exploded in front of Father Kapaun, followed by a volley of mortar and artillery rounds. He was blown off his feet. He sat stunned, his ears ringing. His rosary beads lay on the ground near him. He shook his head and reached out for the beads. Another volley of artillery resounded.

Schuler gunned the Jeep and made a fast U-turn. The Jeep groaned as Schuler cut it too short, causing the trailer to jackknife. He was stuck. A mortar round blew the trailer into scrap metal, knocking the Jeep into the ditch along with its valiant driver.

Father Kapaun shook off his shock and took cover behind a hut wall. He saw Chaplain Mills in the open, hugging the ground. Lieutenant Nardella stood by the side of the bombed-out hut. The lieutenant motioned to Chaplain Mills and said, "Chaplain, get over here! We need to get out of here now!"

Chaplain Mills got up and took a few steps before a mortar round exploded near him. Mills fell to the ground with a scream. Schuler extricated himself from the Jeep, got out of the ditch, and ran across the road. Enemy rifle fire tore up the ground near Schuler, hitting him in the knee. He fell to the ground. Struggling to stand, the PFC limped over to Chaplain Mills, arriving at the same time as Father Kapaun.

Father Kapaun tried to get Chaplain Mill's attention, yelling over the gunfire and explosions going off. "Chaplain, let's get you to safety!"

Chaplain Mills shook his head and said, "I don't think that's going to happen." He motioned toward the ground in front of him.

They all looked down at his leg. His lower left leg had been blown off.

Explosions continued to rock the village and surrounding valley. Lieutenant Nardella arrived on the scene, grabbed Chaplain Mills, and carried him over behind the wall of the bombed-out hut, and laid him on the ground.

"He needs a tourniquet!" Schuler yelled.

"And you don't?" Lieutenant Nardella said.

"Don't worry about me. Let's get the Chaplain taken care of first," Schuler retorted.

"Okay," the lieutenant agreed.

Father Kapaun looked around. He saw the Papa-San dead on the ground nearby, the can of Spam still clutched in his hand. One of the children lay at his feet, dead. Father Kapaun pulled a strap off the bundle he carried, leaned down, and wrapped it tightly around the chaplain's leg in a desperate attempt to stop him from bleeding out.

"I'll never take another leak again as long as I live," Chaplain Mills said breathlessly.

"We need to get him help, pronto!" Nardella urged.

Father Kapaun looked at Schuler and asked, "Any ideas?"

PFC Schuler looked around. The trailer was trashed, but the Jeep seemed still to be in one piece.

"Let me see if I can get the Jeep started again," he said.

Everyone nodded, hopeful he could pull it off. Kapaun said a silent prayer.

PFC Schuler half-ran, half-limped across the road towards the Jeep, bullets tearing up the ground around him. Lieutenant Nardella aimed at an enemy soldier up on the slope above the village who was shooting at Schuler and put three bullets in the enemy's chest before he could strike his intended victim.

Schuler jumped into the Jeep and drove it out of the ditch as Father Kapaun and Lieutenant Nardella picked up Chaplain Mills and carried him across the road towards the Jeep. As they started to get into the Jeep, they heard a 'VIPFFF VIPFFF VIPFFF.'

"What's that sound?" Father Kapaun asked, agitated.

They all looked down the road in time to see numerous .50 caliber bullets rake the road in a pattern headed their way.

"Hit the ditch!" Schuler screamed, jumping from the Jeep and back into the ditch. Kapaun dragged Chaplain Mills over the edge of the vehicle and onto the ground. Nardella helped him drag the chaplain into a thicket of bushes.

Three U.S. Navy Corsair F-4U fighters strafed the valley. The Jeep and trailer went up in a ball of flames. PFC Schuler joined the little group as gunfire continued all around them. Chaplain Mills was in and out of consciousness and Kapaun heard him praying sporadically.

Sergeant Bill Richardson, Corporal Walt Gray, Sergeant Pappy Miller, Sergeant Vincent Doyle, and several more infantrymen on foot appeared suddenly from the surrounding cover, firing on the enemy. Sergeant Richardson looked down at Father Kapaun and company, huddled together in the ditch, and shook his head. He looked back at the men he had walked into the village with and yelled, "Will you peckerheads spread out before you draw more fire?"

Richardson moved forward, some soldiers following behind him, others scattering. Gray looked at the chaplain's leg and gasped. He stepped back and motioned people over to him saying, "Over here! Get the medics!"

Corporal Gray's voice drew enemy submachine gunfire from a nearby hut. He dove for cover, shielding Chaplain Mills at the same time. He waited for a moment, then popped up and returned fire at the hut. He looked down at Chaplain Mills and said, "Hang in there, Chaplain, the calvary's here."

Sergeant Richardson moved down the street, giving hand signals to his men as he surveyed the place. Sergeant Miller took a position against the side of an old burnt car and saw two enemy soldiers some thirty feet away. He took aim and fired, killing both men before they could get a shot off.

Richardson signaled Corporal Gray to check out the hut. Corporal Gray checked his equipment, positioned himself just outside the hut, ready to enter.

Suddenly, from inside the hut, two shots were fired, neither of them hitting the corporal. Then Gray heard several shots inside the hut as if the enemy were shooting at one another.

Corporal Gray pulled the pin on a grenade. He held the grenade in his hand for a couple of seconds before lobbing it into the hut and taking cover.

The grenade exploded, blowing a hole in the back wall of the hut. A boy in the corner was unhurt while his comrades staggered around outside, dazed, trying to get their bearings.

Sergeant Richardson and Sergeant Doyle walked around the back and fired on the two men, killing both.

The boy ran off through a rice paddy. A soldier lifted his gun to shoot the kid when Corporal Gray shook his head at the soldier, stopping him. "He's just a kid. Let him go." The soldier lowered his rifle reluctantly, and the two men watched as the boy sprinted away.

Master Sergeant Richardson marched up to Father Kapaun. "Just what did you think you were doing, Father, stopping at some rinky-dink village? Desperately need to meet the locals?"

Kapaun spoke up confidently. "I was ministering. That's what I do. That's why I'm here."

"To our men! Not to the godless communists," Richardson exploded.

"Bill, if they're godless, it's all the more my responsibility to minister. Besides, the old man made the sign of the cross. There were hungry children," Kapaun argued.

"And now they're dead. Chaplain Mills lost his leg, and my men had to come to the rescue."

"I know. I take responsibility for the incident. But I'd do it again, Bill. You should know that."

"Father, I respect your role here, but when it involves putting my men at risk, then it becomes my responsibility to tell you to mind your own business." Richardson shook his head and walked away.

"God go with you," the priest said softly …

☆ ☆ ☆

Later that night, a medic chopper lifted off under cover of darkness with Chaplain Mills onboard, taking him back to Taegu. There was the sound of enemy machine-gun fire, but the chopper got away clean.

Father Kapaun, PFC Schuler, and Lieutenant Nardella watched the chopper while hunkering down in a foxhole, enemy shells still exploding all around them.

"Patrick, why didn't they airlift you out, too?" Lieutenant Nardella asked.

PFC Schuler looked at his leg and shrugged. "It was like a through and through. Already feeling better." He patted his leg and winced.

Lieutenant Nardella's expression indicated that he wasn't convinced, but it wasn't his call. He shrugged and looked away.

Father Kapaun suddenly put his finger to his lips and shushed them. The voices of enemy soldiers could be heard along with faint explosions from further down the bowling alley, but they couldn't see the enemy from their position.

"Looks like we're here for the night," Father Kapaun whispered.

"You think we're safe?" Schuler asked. He fingered the hole in his pants.

"No one is safe," the lieutenant answered.

"I was asking Father Kapaun, Lieutenant," PFC Schuler said, irritated.

"We'll be fine," Father Kapaun said; then he pulled out his rosary and said a silent prayer, thinking about his first experience with a bullet whizzing past his head. Something he would never forget. It was a split-second life or death situation. He could have lost his faith in that moment or, as happened, he stood and gained his courage with no questioning of his faith.

Chapter 4

August 13, 1950

Ka-San Mountain

The next day, Sergeant Richardson walked the hilltop of the mountain on the east side of the Bowling Alley called Ka-San — the soldiers called it 'Hill 902' — greeting and reassuring each of the many wounded soldiers. Back at the Tabu-dong triage station, Doc Anderson and the nurses were working hard to keep the men who'd been brought in alive. Several men had died in their foxholes, their throats slit during the night. PFC Busatti and Lieutenant Nardella were taking out the dead on stretchers. They stared emotionless at the carnage, shaking their heads. They were in shock and moved mechanically.

"One day you're minding your own business and the next day you wake up too late to keep your throat from being slit," Busatti said. He had to swallow hard to keep from vomiting at the stench and gore around him.

"So true," added the lieutenant as Sergeant Doyle walked over to them.

"What was it the chaplain said in World War Two?" Doyle asked.

"There are no atheists in a foxhole," Busatti said.

"You got that right," Doyle said.

Schuler and Father Kapaun walked together some forty feet behind the three. Kapaun was exhausted from his night in the foxhole and his day given to praying for the dead and wounded. He wondered when he could next get some sleep. Schuler had been relieved of the duty of carrying the dead.

"Damn, I'm starving. We can't stay out in the open like this," PFC Schuler said.

A squadron of F-51 Mustangs roared overhead. They followed the trail of the planes with their eyes. Father Kapaun looked hard into the valley and spotted something orange several hundred yards away.

"You're right. Look, an orange grove. And they're in season," Father Kapaun said. He said a little prayer of thanks.

"Makes for good cover, too," Schuler added, nodding his head. They veered off course slightly, hungrily making their way to the orange grove.

The North Korean teen whom Corporal Gray had let escape the evening before, emerged cautiously from the brush, unseen, watching Father Kapaun and PFC Schuler as they walked by.

As they entered the orange grove, Father Kapaun stumbled over an army M-1 carbine and picked it up. Schuler watched him and a smile appeared on his face.

"I thought you couldn't carry a weapon," Schuler said.

"I can carry one. Can even shoot the eyes out of a snake if I wanted to. I was a pretty good shot on the farm in Kansas. I just usually choose not to carry one. But if it's a question of a Red sending me to heaven or me sending him to hell ... let's just say I feel like I'm needed here right now."

Schuler laughed and said, "Good to hear."

Father Kapaun struggled to chamber a round with the dust-covered cocking handle. It finally slid forward. He pointed the rifle at the ground and pulled the trigger. Nothing, the whole firing mechanism was clogged.

"Not much of a weapon anyway. More like a big stick," Father Kapaun joked.

They walked deeper into the grove and began loading up on oranges. Schuler pulled his shirt out and made a hammock for the fruit. Father Kapaun saw a big, ripe orange just out of reach. Using the carbine, he knocked the orange free, and it fell into his hand. A twig snapped behind them. Father Kapaun reeled around, rifle in hand, and found himself face to face with the North Korean teen soldier. He put his finger on the trigger.

Schuler saw the stand-off. The only weapon he had in his hand was an orange. It was a tense moment. A jet engine roared above them, growing louder and louder as the fighter jet screamed past them. The Korean boy hit the deck, scared for his life. Father Kapaun did not flinch. He motioned the boy to stand. The boy stood without his rifle. Schuler swooped down and picked it up. The oranges in his shirt rolled to the ground. Father Kapaun looked the boy over and tossed him the orange he had pulled from the tree.

As the kid devoured the orange, Schuler picked up the boy's rifle and said, "Wow, he's one sad sack."

"He knows he's a kid, not meant to kill people. He was seeking mercy at the sign of the cross," Father Kapaun replied.

"Or at the sight of your gun," Schuler offered.

The boy smiled and bowed his head, awash in new happiness. Schuler pointed his new rifle at the kid and said, "Move it or lose it, kiddo."

The boy walked off quickly, Schuler following with a gun pointed at him, Father Kapaun bringing up the rear, the carbine slung over his shoulder, carrying Schuler's rifle. He eagerly munched on an orange and wondered on this blessing.

☆ ☆ ☆

Father Kapaun and PFC Patrick Schuler arrived at the triage station in the village of Tabu-dong, near at the southern end of the valley, with the boy soldier at the tip of his own gun. Two MPs watched them march the boy into camp and rushed over to help.

The closest MP assessed the situation and said, "We've got him."

Father Kapaun held his hands up and handed over the M-1. He didn't want to interfere with the military police. He nodded at the MP. The two MPs grabbed the boy by the arms and started marching him off to a fate unknown. Father Kapaun and Schuler continued to watch as the MPs walked away with the boy. Kapaun said a prayer for the boy. After all, this was war: no place for kids. He'd seen his share of dead young men and women, children, along the way. He had to believe it was God's plan.

After the MPs passed from sight, they looked up at the triage station before them.

"After you, Father," Schuler said with a slight bow and a gentle wave of his hand.

"I think you may need this place more than me," Father Kapaun replied.

They walked into the triage station together.

☆ ☆ ☆

Father Kapaun looked for Chaplain Mills as he and Schuler walked around inside the triage station. He noticed PFC Schuler was still limping and said, "You should probably get that leg looked at now, Patrick."

"I'm okay, Father," Schuler replied, pounding his fist against his leg. He winced a little, trying to hide the pain. Father Kapaun gave him an incredulous look. PFC Schuler laughed and said, "Okay, I'll see what they can do for me."

He quickly made his way over to Nurse Mary who was standing nearby, writing on a chart.

Mary saw him approaching, noticed him limping, and looked decidedly concerned.

"Can I help you, Patrick?" Nurse Mary asked. She replaced the chart on the bottom rung of a soldier's bed.

"I sure hope so, Mary. I seem to have been shot."

Schuler showed Mary the bullet hole in his pants leg. She nodded, patted the top of an empty stretcher, and said, "Hop on up. Let me get a look at that. But you're going to have to lose the trousers first."

Schuler let his pants fall to the ground before clumsily climbing onto the stretcher.

"When did you get shot?" Nurse Mary inquired. She began to probe the wound. Schuler winced.

"Yesterday. Nothing too bad," he said bravely. "Went right through. Father Kapaun said I should get it checked out though."

Mary gently shook her head at Schuler and said, "All I can say is I'm glad you listened to him. It may not be bad now, but if it gets infected, you could lose that leg."

Schuler, suddenly looking worried, asked, "Do you think I could really ...?"

Nurse Mary held a hand up to stop him and said, "Don't worry. You're in good hands. I've got this."

He breathed a sigh of relief and said, "Thank you, Mary."

She looked up from his leg and smiled, "That's what I'm here for."

Nearby, Doc Anderson and Nurse Eva worked on Chaplain Mills who was connected to a morphine drip, his eyes closed. Father Kapaun walked over.

"Hey, Doc. How's the chaplain doing?" Father Kapaun asked, keeping his voice low.

"He's in good spirits. That's something," Doc replied.

Chaplain Mills opened his eyes. He saw Father Kapaun standing there and smiled.

"Is that the cowboy priest from Kansas I hear?" Chaplain Mills said.

Father Kapaun walked closer so Chaplain Mills could see him more clearly. He looked down on Chaplain Mills and said, "Thought I'd better come check on you. Glad to see you're awake."

"Bless you, Father," Chaplain Mills replied, touched that Father Kapaun had taken the time to seek him out.

Father Kapaun made the sign of the cross, blessing the chaplain. He smiled and nodded at Doc Anderson and Nurse Eva.

"Nice seeing you, Father," Nurse Eva said.

"You, too, Eva."

Doc Anderson continued working on Chaplain Mills whose leg was just a stump, bandaged at the knee. Father Kapaun looked at the chaplain's leg and forced a smile. It still wasn't easy to see men and women who were seriously injured. No amount of time in the field would make that seem normal.

"My days of blessing the mass graves of children are over. No more combat boots for me, thank you," Chaplain Mills said.

"It was an honor to serve by your side. Peace be with you," Father Kapaun said.

Chaplain Mills managed to smile and said, "Think I'll get me a nice pair of fuzzy slippers when I get home. Well, one slipper anyway."

Chaplain Mills looked lost, wishing he hadn't spoken about slippers, creating an awkward moment. After a few seconds, he asked, "How's that Gray fella doing?"

Father Kapaun looked confused and said, "Excuse me?"

"Corporal Walt Gray? Ralph Nardella carried me to safety and Walt got the medics in and ordered the chopper that brought me here. What a team!"

Father Kapaun smiled, remembering how efficiently Corporal Gray had acted while they had all been stuck in such a precarious position.

"I'm so happy they got you out of there. The Corporal is fine. If there's anything I can do for you just let me know," Father Kapaun said.

"Actually, there is. Ralph's been by to check on me already. Good man. I blessed him myself. But I haven't seen Corporal Gray. I'm afraid I won't be here much longer. They're going to ship me out. If you could find Walt and bless him for me, I would be eternally grateful."

Father Kapaun nodded, considering the request.

"The troops have been split up so much I don't know where anyone is anymore, but I will do my best to find him and bless him for you. You get some rest and get well," Father Kapaun said.

"Thank you, Father," Chaplain Mills replied, looking pleased.

Father Kapaun smiled, gently squeezed Chaplain Mill's hand, and headed toward the triage station exit feeling weighted down by Mills' future.

Father Kapaun walked out of the triage station alone. A few soldiers milled around outside, but otherwise, the place looked deserted. He wondered about that because the triage tent had been pretty full. He expected others to be visiting their compatriots. He lit his pipe and walked around, thinking about what Chaplain Mills had asked him to do. He saw Lieutenant Bob Wood walk by.

"Excuse me, son. Would you happen to know where Corporal Walt Gray is?" Father Kapaun asked.

"I believe he's on Hill 829, Father," Wood replied.

Father Kapaun looked confused. He wrinkled his brow and asked, "Where would that be?"

Lieutenant Wood pulled a map out of his pocket and showed Father Kapaun where Hill 829 was in relation to where they were. Father Kapaun studied the map for a moment, before nodding his head at Wood and said, "Thank you, son."

"Happy to help," the lieutenant said cheerfully and walked off, stuffing the map back into his pocket.

Lieutenant Mike Dowe pulled into the parking area nearby and parked a Jeep filled with a few soldiers including Sergeant Vincent Doyle.

Father Kapaun walked over to Dowe. By the time he reached him most of the rest of the men had jumped out of the Jeep and had gone their separate ways.

Father Kapaun ran his fingers over his hair and said, "Mike, I was wondering if you could help me? I'm looking for the best way to get to hill 829."

"Of course, Father. Can I ask why on earth you want to go there?" Dowe asked.

"I'm looking for Corporal Walt Gray. I have a blessing I need to bestow upon him for Chaplain Mills."

"Okay, Father. But Walt's not on hill 829. He's on Hill 902," Lieutenant Dowe responded.

Father Kapaun looked him in the eye, even more confused than before.

The lieutenant smiled and said, "I'd be happy to take you there myself, Father."

Father Kapaun breathed a slow sigh of relief and said, "That's very kind of you, Mike."

"Mind if I tag along?" Sergeant Doyle asked.

"The more the merrier," Father Kapaun replied.

They chuckled and climbed into the Jeep. Lieutenant Dowe fired up the engine and off they drove.

☆ ☆ ☆

Sergeant Bill Richardson, Corporal Walt Gray, and Sergeant Pappy Miller walked along the pathways on the ridgeline of Hill 902 along with dozens of other soldiers. Everyone trod carefully and stayed low to the ground. Richardson looked in every direction, last around a large tree, checking for enemy movement; the area looked clear.

"Take five everyone," he said.

The other soldiers took seats on the ground while Richardson, Gray, and Miller huddled together nearby. Sergeant Richardson pulled a pack of cigarettes from his pocket; then he realized it was empty. He made a face, firmly squished the empty pack in his hand, and threw it on the ground.

"Want a smoke?" Miller asked, reaching for his own pack.

"Nah, I should probably quit anyway," Richardson replied.

"Just wish it wasn't so damned hot," Gray said, sweat dripping down his forehead and into his shirt.

Miller glanced at Gray and nodded in agreement as he wiped streams of sweat from his own forehead. It was excruciatingly hot. Sergeant Miller looked back at Sergeant Richardson and said, "Come on, trade you some smokes for some fruit or some of your more edible c-rations."

Sergeant Richardson shook his head at Sergeant Miller and said, "Tell you what, Pappy, help us take this hill and I promise you a full rack of BBQ ribs at your choice of any of Seoul's finest restaurants."

Sergeant Miller's face lit up. "You got yourself a deal!"

Sergeant Richardson looked at Corporal Gray and said, "Walt, the squads should be separated by twenty yards. I'll show you how to ..." Sergeant Richardson scrunched up his face. After a minute, Sergeant Richardson said, "You okay, Walt?"

Corporal Gray swayed a bit as if he were about to fall over, but he nodded. The others thought he looked as if he were about to faint. He said, "Think I just need to sit down for a minute." He walked over and sat on a tree stump, his head in his hands.

Sergeant Richardson took his helmet off and wiped the sweat from his forehead. Suddenly, he heard a familiar, whirring banshee noise coming from somewhere and looked all around, his eyes growing wide. The noise got louder and louder.

Sergeant Richardson looked at Corporal Gray and was about to say, "Take cover!" when, boom, a mortar round exploded right on top of Corporal Gray. The stump disappeared and was replaced by the two halves of Walt's bloody body and a smoking crater.

Sergeant Richardson yelled, "Jesus Christ! Fan the hell out!"

He looked at the crater for another second, not believing his eyes. Then he jumped into action as the men took up positions establishing a perimeter and taking cover in preparation for either an imminent enemy assault or more incoming artillery fire.

☆ ☆ ☆

Nurse Deborah walked towards the triage station. Several soldiers and MPs watched as she walked by, craning their necks to get a better look at her attractive face and figure.

PFC Joe Ramirez saw her approaching, stopped, and gave an indiscreet wolf whistle. She stopped, looked at him, shook her head in disapproval.

"Joe, don't you know where we are?" Deborah scolded.

She started to walk by him, but he stepped out, blocking her way.

"Sorry. Couldn't help myself. Not good in front of beautiful women," Ramirez said somewhat apologetically.

"I'm not beautiful, Joe," Deborah said, blushing.

"So, they don't have mirrors where you're staying?" Ramirez teased.

She laughed and said, "Cut it out."

"I'm just saying, I think you're the bee's knees, and I'd love to go out with you sometime," Ramirez said, his eyes full of adoration and boyish hope.

"You're not afraid I'd sting you, being the bee's knees and all?" she replied, teasing him back.

They both laughed, just a little, wary of being overheard by the others nearby.

"I'm afraid you already have. Thankfully, you're a nurse so maybe you can put something on it," he said, a big smile on his face.

She looked him up and down, looking undecided. Then she said, "I don't know what to say. I mean, you are cute and all, but I doubt we'll get a chance to go to the movies and hold hands or anything."

"Just tell me I've got a shot and I'll figure something out."

She smiled and thought about it for a quick second. "Maybe."

She walked off. He watched her walk away, unable to see her face anymore but enjoying the tight wiggle in her walk.

"I'll take a maybe. It's a helluva lot better than a no," he replied, just loud enough for her to hear him.

Deborah did not look back. She walked through the triage station doors, smiling.

☆ ☆ ☆

Nurse Deborah walked into the triage station, still smiling. She'd not been hit on like that for quite some time and appreciated the attentions of the handsome young private. Korea was a nightmare and anything to pretend it didn't exist was okay by her.

Nurse Mary noticed her smiling and wondered what was going on. "Hey, Deb, what has you in such a good mood?" she asked.

"Oh, nothing really," Deborah said, walking off towards the central unit, still not able to wipe the smile off her face. She didn't need to be teased by the other women. This would be her little secret for now.

Eva and Sally joined Mary.

"What was that all about?" Sally asked Mary.

"Heck if I know," Mary replied, shaking her head.

"You think she's got a guy after her?" Eva asked.

"I wouldn't be surprised," Sally said. "She'd be quite a catch."

"If she does, all I can say is good for her," Mary added and the three of them watched Deborah filling out paperwork, looking happier than they'd ever seen her look before.

☆ ☆ ☆

Lieutenant Mike Dowe drove towards Hill 902. Father Kapaun sat in the Jeep's passenger seat, enduring the bumpy ride while Sergeant Vincent Doyle rode in the back, bopping his head back and forth like he was listening to music inside his mind.

"So, tell me, Father, what would make you decide to join the Army and put your life in danger like this?" Mike asked. He navigated the holes and ruts in the trail expertly.

"I go where God sends me. This isn't my first time at war," Father Kapaun replied.

Mike wrinkled his forehead. He asked, "What do you mean it's not your first time at war?"

"I was a chaplain in World War II. I've seen my share of death and helped where I could. It was never easy, but I feel like I made a difference. Well, God made a difference. I just tagged along," Father Kapaun told him.

"I'm sure you did make a difference, but why'd you come back, knowing how difficult it had been?" Mike asked, more curious than ever.

"Oddly enough, it was a newsreel that got my attention and made me want to come back," Father Kapaun replied.

Mike looked surprised and asked, "A newsreel?"

"That's right. I was at the theater with a friend, and they played a newsreel and in it, they said Kim Il Sung was the self-proclaimed Great Leader of North Korea and he'd kicked out all non-communists from his country, aligned himself with the communists, and had the North Korean People's Army preparing for an armed crusade to unify the country. I went to Bishop Carroll that very day and asked him to allow me to return to service. There's no place for more Communism in the world."

"How'd your family take that news?" Mike asked.

"They supported me, although I'm sure they weren't happy about it. Especially my mother." Father Kapaun was lost in deep thought as if reliving a memory. He began to remember the day he had told his family he was going back to war:

☆ ☆ ☆

He was sitting at the breakfast table with his parents, Bessie and Enos, in their farmhouse outside of Pilsen, Kansas. He looked at his parents in his memory. No one looked happy, including himself. He was just thirty-three years old and had been to war once already.

They were dressed in working clothes and he was wearing his dress uniform, ready to leave within the hour. In his memory, he looked around the familiar room again. He saw the pots hanging over the stove, the neatly laid table, the cupboards filled with his mother's dishes. Outside, he could see the outbuildings where the animals stayed, the chicken coop where he'd gathered eggs for his mother most of his life.

His father, a small, gracious man, gave him a wide-eyed, earnest look and said, "Don't worry about our corn crop, son. We'll survive. Got plenty of wheat harvested this year."

He smiled at his father and said, "I remember when it would rain during harvest and we'd get stuck with the binder." He dug into the eggs his mother had prepared, fresh from the chicken coop.

His father smiled back and said, "That's Kansas weather for you. Pray for rain, you get a flood."

They laughed.

His mother, Bessie, looked irritated and alarmed. "Do we have to talk about the crops? Our son's going off to war. Again."

No one talked for a few moments. Kapaun drank his black coffee. Bessie managed a fake smile for a moment, and then she broke the silence by addressing her son. "You do look downright handsome in that Army dress uniform, Emil." She picked up her coffee, her hands shaking a bit.

"Thank you, Mother," he replied.

"Guess we have to call you Chaplain Kapaun again," Bessie said. "As if Burma wasn't far enough. And now this Korea, wherever that is."

"Or Captain. Don't forget his rank," Enos chimed in.

"That's true. Captain Kapaun. I like the sound of that," Bessie said with just a hint of pride in her voice.

Bessie's mouth looked like it was trying to smile, yet her eyes looked like they were ready to cry. Enos reached over and flicked away a tear.

Emil covered his mother's hand with his own and said, "Actually, I prefer Father Kapaun."

Enos smiled and said, "Father Kapaun. I like the sound of that, son. It's enough to make your old man proud."

But Bessie still looked more worried than she was proud.

"I'm going to be fine, Mother. I've done this before. God will watch over me."

Bessie nodded and said, "I know. I know. Just promise me you'll come back in one piece."

"I'll do everything I can, but I can't promise that."

Enos glared at his son, telling him with his eyes that he said the wrong thing.

He took another bite of his eggs and homemade bread and said, "Um, this is delicious, Mother."

Bessie tried to smile, but it was too hard for her filled as she was with doubt.

Father Kapaun gently smiled at the memory, but he was suddenly pulled back into the present moment when he heard Mike yell. Gunfire erupted all around them. Mike swerved the Jeep back and forth trying not to get hit whilst getting out of the area.

"Hang on, Father. We're under some heavy fire," Mike said, looking around.

Vincent fired his rifle from the back seat, not that he could hit anything, as Mike maneuvered the Jeep like a race car driver.

To their right, Mike saw Richardson with his section firing at the enemy and drove in his direction. Father Kapaun lowered his head and silently prayed.

Gunfire was blazing all around the sergeant. They all leaped out of the Jeep. Sergeant Pappy Miller was engaging the enemy, taking out an enemy soldier as Mike and Vincent joined him, rounds flaring. Father Kapaun ran toward the group, hoping he might be of use.

Nearby, an American soldier was shot through the eye and fell to the ground, bleeding badly. Father Kapaun immediately ran over to him, kneeling down to ascertain his condition, already praying over the boy as his lifeforce faded away.

Behind them, Mike located and fired at the enemy infantryman who had shot the soldier in the eye, taking him out and feeling some fleeting solace in meting out such swift revenge.

A squad of North Koreans charged toward the GIs.

Sergeant Richardson yelled at his men, "Rally Soldiers! Don't let these gooks win!"

He fired his weapon repeatedly, taking out enemy after enemy. Another two North Korean soldiers charged forward and were cut down by Mike and Pappy. The remaining enemy soldiers ran off; most of them were too far away for the Americans to even shoot.

Still kneeling, Sergeant Richardson yelled at his men, "Stay alert, men! Some of them may still be alive. If they move, shoot 'em!" The situation was too fluid to show mercy. He cautiously stood, crouched over, and walked towards the enemy location.

The majority of the men followed closely behind, keeping their heads down, looking all around for anything that moved. Dead soldiers lay all over the area. The men walked carefully through the woods, checking for heartbeats. Sergeant Richardson noticed two enemy soldiers on the ground, barely breathing. He put a bullet in both men's heads, ending their lives. Was it compassion? Maybe but there again …

☆ ☆ ☆

Later, after taking care to make sure all of the enemy soldiers were dead and that there were no more in the immediate vicinity, Sergeant Richardson and the rest of the platoon made their way back to the position they had occupied up on the ridgeline before everything had gone crazy.

The sergeant looked over at the spot where Corporal Walt Gray had been killed and sat down, shaking his head in disbelief. So many things had happened at once that he had not had even a second to grieve the loss of a man who had been possibly his best soldier, so he did so now, silently.

Father Kapaun was busy giving last prayers to the downed soldiers. Several soldiers surrounded him, most looking at the same spot Richardson was looking at, many making the sign of the cross; each said his own goodbye.

Father Kapaun finished giving last rites to the last of the most severely wounded U.S. servicemen and looked over at Sergeant Richardson. Seeing him standing there, looking as if he'd lost his best friend, Kapaun got to his feet and went to join him.

"I can't believe all the bodies lying dead here on this beautiful mountainside. It's downright crazy," Father Kapaun said.

Sergeant Richardson, his grieving interrupted, looked over at Father Kapaun, nodded, and said, "You're right. It is crazy." He paused and studied Kapaun. "Hey, Father, I appreciate everything you did here but, just curious, what made you come out here in the first place?"

"I am looking for Corporal Walt Gray. I promised Chaplain Mills I would bless him. I haven't seen him though. Maybe I'm on the wrong hill."

Sergeant Richardson dropped his head, shaking it steadily from side to side, unable to look Father Kapaun in the eyes.

"I'm afraid Walt didn't make it, Father," he replied.

Richardson nodded towards the spot where Walt's charred remains lay. "He was sitting right there when a mortar took him out." The crater continued to smoke.

Lieutenant Dowe and Sergeant Doyle looked over, their eyes bulging. They'd already seen a lot of death, but this was beyond gruesome. Walt Gray had been well-liked and respected — a soldier's soldier. It was an image of war that all of them would try to forget. Yet, none would ever forget what they saw that day.

Father Kapaun looked over, not believing what he was seeing. He shuddered and looked away. He'd been in the field for a long time; this shouldn't affect him, but he took it far harder than he expected to. Sergeant Miller put a hand on the father's shoulder and said, "Walt was a good man. He didn't deserve to die like that."

"Does anyone?" Father Kapaun replied, shaking his head.

Sergeant Richardson stood, seething with a wave of palpable anger, far angrier than Father Kapaun had ever seen him before, and said, "The peckerheads that killed him do. That's for damned sure."

"You can say that again," Sergeant Miller said, spitting vengeance.

Father Kapaun continued to look at poor Walt's body split in two and said, "I'll pray for Walt's family. Chaplain Mills may have lost his leg, but at least he didn't lose his life. That was because of the work you're doing. He was especially grateful to Walt. I understand he fought very bravely, and I am sure he will be remembered fondly."

Sergeant Richardson nodded, still incensed, and said, "That he will, Father. That he will."

Chapter 5

August 14, 1950

Nurses' Quarters

Tabu-dong

F our cots were positioned closely together in the tent that served as the nurses' living quarters. Nurse Sally was alone in the room, lying on her cot, absentmindedly flipping through a magazine, a field lantern lit behind her. It had been a long, hard day, like most of their days, but finally, she had been allowed some downtime.

Eva walked into the tent, her brow furrowed and her mouth in a frown. Sally looked up from her magazine and could immediately tell from the look on Eva's face that something was wrong; yes, something was terribly wrong.

"Hey, Eva? Everything okay?" Sally asked.

Eva walked silently around the small room, opening and closing her mouth as if she had something to tell Sally making no sound. She felt like she was about to explode, but she was completely unsure of how to proceed.

"Not really," Eva said, trying to work up some courage.

Sally knew Eva was holding something back and wanted to say something to put her at ease. "Eva, if there's something I can do to …"

Eva stopped her, saying "No!" and turned her head away.

Sally looked more worried than before and said, "Whatever it is, you can tell me, Eva. I'm always here for you."

The emotion welling up inside, Eva looked like she was about to cry and said, "I ... I just found out some horrible news."

The moment was interrupted as Mary and Deborah entered the tent, laughing.

"Boy, what a day," Mary said.

"You can say that again," Deborah agreed.

Mary and Deborah walked over to their beds, slipping out of their nurse's uniforms. Mary looked over, felt the tension in the room, and asked, "Did we interrupt something?"

Deborah, ever curious, looked over to see what she missed.

"Eva was about to tell me some news," Sally said.

Deborah cocked her face and inquired, "What kind of news?"

"It was really just for Sally," Eva said.

"I hope you're not confessing your love for her, Eva, because that would be awkward," Deborah said, laughing. No one laughed with her.

Sally rolled her eyes, looked at Eva. She sat up in bed and said, "Come on, Eva. Just tell me for Christ's sake! You're starting to get me worried."

Eva hesitated for a moment. All eyes were on her. Finally, she blurted, "It's Walt!"

Sally looked confused. "What about him?"

Eva hesitated another second; then she said, "Walt was killed today."

Immediately, Sally's face went white and she dropped the magazine. It made a swooshing noise. Everyone looked at Sally as if time had stopped.

"Are you sure?" Sally whimpered. Tears filled her eyes.

Eva nodded. "I just heard about it. I'm really sorry." She started to sob.

Eva sat on the edge of Sally's cot, leaned over, and hugged her. Mary and Deborah walked over and hugged Sally, too.

"Walt was a great guy and I know how much you liked each other," Deborah said.

Sally nodded, unable to find her voice. She wiped the tears from her eyes, but they continued rolling down her face.

"He really was a good guy. I can't think of a single person who didn't like him. I'm so sorry for your loss," Mary said.

"I really, really liked him," Sally said, the tears flowing. They all four hugged, tears streaming down their faces as the girls continued to comfort Sally.

☆☆☆

The next day Nurse Sally stood next to Father Kapaun inside a tent filled with stretchers, each containing a dead soldier covered by a poncho as Army personnel attended to the identification process. The dead had their dog tags tied around their right big toe.

Sally was a mess inside and knew she looked it. She wore no make-up, her eyes and nose were red, and it looked like she'd slept in her clothes.

Sally and Father Kapaun looked down at Corporal Gray's bodily remains, the poncho removed to expose only his face, the only part of him that had not been sliced in half. Sally could barely look at Walt. She tried to remember him as he had been two days before.

"Glory be to the Father and to the Son and to the Holy Spirit. As it was in the beginning, it is now and ever shall be, a world without end. Amen," Father Kapaun said. He held his hands together in prayer a moment longer.

"Amen," Sally said softly, tears still rolling down her cheeks.

"He was a special man. A hero to all," Father Kapaun said. He placed his hand on her shoulder, comforting her sobs.

"Thank you, Father," Sally said.

He turned and gently hugged Sally for a few moments. Then he watched her walk from the tent. She was partially bent over, and her arms were wrapped around her body. He paused for a moment, looking back down at Corporal Gray's face before covering him up with the poncho and moving on to the next soldier so that he could bless him, too. He knew that in war, a chaplain's work is never done.

Chapter 6

October 11

Kumchon

On September 15, a U.S. Marines force made a surprise amphibious landing at the strategic port of Inchon, on the west coast of Korea, about 100 miles south of the 38th parallel and 25 miles from Seoul. The landings threw the North Korean Army into disarray and heralded the start of the U.S. 8th Army's breakout from the Pusan Perimeter lead by the 1st Cavalry Division.

PFC Schuler drove the Jeep as the long 1st Cavalry convoy crossed the 38th parallel going north and wound their way past the North Korean border, meaning the Americans were definitely on the offensive at last. Father Kapaun and Sergeant Vincent Doyle rode in the Jeep. Doyle broke out a bottle of Seagram's 7 whiskey and said, "Remember this day, men. We're making history!" He took a swig and passed it around. Even Father Kapaun had a taste.

As they passed a tree to the side of the road, they all saw the body of a North Korean officer hanging from it. His face was black and green, his clothes almost in shreds. Schuler looked at Father Kapaun and happily remarked, "I don't think we're in Kansas anymore, Father!"

Father Kapaun blessed the dead Korean as he remained seated in the speeding Jeep.

On October 9, the division's 7th Cavalry Regiment crossed the Yesong River and began its rapid advance around the west of the enemy pocket. The 5th and 8th Cavalry Regiments remained to the east of the river to complete the encirclement of Kumchon on October 13th.

Sporadic gunfire and explosions from mortar rounds had been heard all morning by the soldiers standing outside the battalion aid station south of Kumchon, South Korea. Several GIs diligently filled empty ammo boxes with dirt and stacked them as high as they could in order to protect the aid station against a potential enemy attack.

Father Kapaun stood in front of a nearby Jeep where he had set up an altar on the hood. He planned to conduct the mass for his faithful flock when the opportunity presented.

Out of nowhere, a high-explosive tank round hit a nearby ammo truck, and it exploded. Everyone hit the dirt, including Father Kapaun, just before another truck exploded close by. Sergeant Miller shot one of several enemy soldiers approaching the aid station, while Lieutenant Dowe's squad fired mortar shells at an enemy tank, eventually hitting the engine deck and crippling the tank's engine. The tank's crew bailed and were allowed to surrender.

PFCs Schuler and Ramirez moved closer to the action, both with new M3 submachine guns in hand, and they managed to shoot the other enemy soldiers. With the situation stabilized, Sergeant Richardson, infuriated, knelt nearby, yelling into a radio mic. He took the microphone he was speaking into and threw it to the ground. Father Kapaun, who had just lit his pipe with shaky hands, noticed the sergeant kneeling, looking angry. He approached him.

"Bill, something I can help with?" Father Kapaun asked.

"I doubt it, Father."

"Try me?"

Richardson sighed, glanced around at everything going on before eyeing Father Kapaun.

"It's Tibor. I sent him and Peter up to do some forward recon and they're trapped up there."

"I've seen Tibor fight. He can find his way out of 'most anything," Father Kapaun replied, trying to offer encouragement.

Sergeant Richardson shook his head and said, "Not this time, Father. They can hardly move. They're pinned down good."

"Then let's go get them," Father Kapaun replied, standing bolt upright, smoking pipe in hand.

A bullet hit his pipe, cutting it in half. He dropped the other half and fell to the ground himself. He looked around and then picked up his pipe, and put both parts of it into his shirt pocket.

"Seems like someone wants you to stop smoking," Richardson said.

They laughed weakly.

"Where're we headed?" Father Kapaun asked. He fingered the pipe in his pocket.

"You still wanna go after nearly getting your ass shot off?" Sergeant Richardson asked, astounded by Father Kapaun's courage. Though he wondered if it was really recklessness.

"Of course. What, you think it's any safer here? Let's go save these men while we still can," Father Kapaun said.

The sergeant frowned, realizing he was probably right, and said, "All right, but keep your head down, Father."

Several more bullets zinged past them. Father Kapaun turned his head and watched them hit the ground. "You got it," Father Kapaun said, blessing himself before taking off with Sergeant Richardson.

☆ ☆ ☆

Nearly an hour later, after carefully making their way past the enemy's defensive position, Sergeant Richardson and Father Kapaun maneuvered through a bombed-out neighborhood on the streets of Kumchon, keeping low to the ground, making the best use of the cover offered by the rubble and remaining structures. Distant small-arms fire, artillery barrages, and tank fire were constant.

"Which way?" Father Kapaun asked.

Sergeant Richardson looked around, trying to get his bearings among the desolation. Nodding towards a bombed-out general store, he said, "Through there."

Father Kapaun looked at the bombed-out store and began to have doubts. The entire area looked like it could be filled with enemy soldiers who could mow them down in seconds, but he knew they must rescue Rubin and Busatti. He nodded at Sergeant Richardson, letting him know he was ready.

Sergeant Richardson immediately took off running, Father Kapaun following closely behind. They had not gotten fifteen feet when sniper rounds began to ping off the street around them, quickly followed by the chatter of a machine-gun. Richardson returned fire at the enemy, taking out two of them while at a full run as Father Kapaun stayed with him. They dove into the bombed-out store, bullets ricocheting all around.

Picking himself up, Richardson quickly ran to the back of the store to escape the gunfire. He needed to determine how close they were to Rubin and Busatti. He looked out the back alley. Father

Kapaun caught up with him. Richardson shook his head in frustration.

"I just don't know where they are," he said quietly.

An enemy soldier came around the corner of the building and rushed at Sergeant Richardson, a bayonet fixed to his rifle. Father Kapaun's heart skipped a beat as he saw the man. He was sure the soldier was going to run Richardson through. Sergeant Richardson saw the man just in time, sidestepped, grabbed the man from behind, and, in one swift motion, snapped the man's neck.

Father Kapaun looked impressed. "Wow, I can't believe you took him out like that. I didn't even see him until he was practically on top of you."

"Yeah, neither did I," Sergeant Richardson said, looking out the back again, breathing a quiet sigh of relief, and shaking his head at his narrow escape.

Father Kapaun joined him as they both searched for signs of the two PFCs After a few moments, Sergeant Richardson said, "Damn. Where are they?"

Father Kapaun scanned the horizon and noticed a hand, half-hidden, clutching an American helmet on a disabled M24 tank in a field nearby. He nodded towards the tank. "What's that, Bill?"

Sergeant Richardson stared, not having much hope. Then he smiled. With excitement in his voice, he said, "By God, you found them, Father! I just hope we can get to them in time."

Father Kapaun nodded, looking around outside. It was a good seventy-five yards to the tank in an open field called Riverfront Park. It may have been closer to a hundred yards and clearly, snipers were active in the area.

"Let's do this," Father Kapaun said.

"All right, let's go," Richardson agreed.

They ran towards the disabled tank as fast as they could. They had barely gotten halfway when two F-80C Shooting Star fighter-bomber jets flew towards them from the north, dropping their pairs of 1000 pound bombs. The bombs exploded behind Richardson and Father Kapaun, utterly demolishing the building they had just been standing in and several others nearby.

They stopped and dropped to the ground behind a tree to avoid the blast and rubble that was thrown in all directions by the bombing run. Once the chaos died down, they looked around carefully and then back at the demolished store. Sergeant Richardson shook his head. "That was a close one."

Father Kapaun nodded. "Think it would've hurt a bit more than getting a pipe shot out of your hand."

The sergeant laughed shortly and said, "Ain't that the truth. Come on, Father, let's rescue these men."

Father Kapaun nodded again, and they resumed their run across the field towards the knocked-out tank.

PFCs Rubin and Busatti stood together behind the disabled tank. Busatti held his helmet out to the side in a desperate attempt to be seen. They watched as Richardson and Father Kapaun ran towards them. Peter looked gleeful.

"It worked! They're coming to rescue us!" Busatti said.

"I just hope they don't get killed trying," Rubin said, his brow furrowed.

"Good point," Busatti said. He quickly sank to the ground.

They both looked at Busatti's bloody leg; a bullet had torn a hole through his trousers and into his knee.

Peter Busatti suddenly looked less gleeful as he glanced around, surveying the area.

Sergeant Richardson and Father Kapaun were halfway between the tree and the tank when a North Korean tank commander popped out of the hatch of a knocked-out tank, holding a submachine gun. He began wildly spraying the area with bullets.

Sergeant Richardson and Father Kapaun hit the dirt. The submachine gun fire stopped. The tank gunner was staring at the gun, furiously hitting it on the side.

Calmly and in a show of confidence, Rubin stepped out from behind the tank and fired a single shot at the tank gunner; the bullet hit him in the center of the forehead, killing him instantly.

Sergeant Richardson and Father Kapaun saw the enemy fall over dead, jumped up, and made their way to the two men who were now crouching down behind the tank.

"Thought we were done for," Rubin said.

Sergeant Richardson smiled and said, "I'd never let that happen. Let's get back to camp before the good Father's luck runs out."

"Right behind you," Busatti said. He staggered up from the ground, his back rested against the side of the tank.

Rubin looked at Father Kapaun and said, "You never stop with the mitzvahs, do you?"

The two men grinned at one another. The others looked baffled.

"Are you okay, Peter?" Father Kapaun asked, looking at Peter's wound.

"I'm fine. It's nothing serious. Just makes it a little hard to move."

"Don't worry, we've got you," Father Kapaun said, nodding at Tibor to help.

With Bill in the lead, rifle shouldered at the ready and constantly scanning for any sign of the enemy, Father Kapaun and

Tibor helped Peter walk as they made their way away from the disabled tank and back toward the command post.

☆ ☆ ☆

When they arrived back at the battalion aid station, everyone looking relieved. Even Busatti looked less scared, though he was still in considerable pain. Father Kapaun waved to the three as the trio made its way into the aid station to get Busatti's leg seen to. He wandered over to the supply room tent, found some heavy-duty adhesive tape, pulled his broken pipe out of his shirt pocket, and quickly put the two pieces back together.

Back at his own tent, he found some paper and a pen, took a seat, lit his pipe, and began slowly puffing on it. He heard distant explosions and gunfire in the background, far away from him yet constant. But it had become normal to him at this point, and soon he barely noticed it at all. He sighed gently and began writing a letter, a letter home.

☆ ☆ ☆

Bessie Kapaun walked through the kitchen, reading the letter, and laughing. Enos stood nearby, watching her, happy to see a smile on her face.

"What's it say?" Enos asked.

"I've only read it four times, so I haven't memorized it yet," Bessie replied. She laughed at her own joke.

"Mind if I read it?"

He tried to snatch the letter, but she turned her body to keep it away from him.

"I'll read it to you," she said. She sat at the table where she sipped on a cup of tea and ran her hand through her hair before starting to read.

"Fine." He sat on the other side of the table.

She looked at the letter, smiled, and began reading it aloud.

"Dear Mom and Dad, I hope things are going well with you and at the farm. I know Kansas weather can be a lot to deal with, and I wish I were there to help, but it's hard to be in two places at one time. You know that I felt I was needed here. When God calls, one must answer. I know you understand even if you don't love me being here.

Things are progressing nicely over here. With a little luck, this whole thing will be over by the time you receive this letter. That's my hope, anyway. I've met some great people here who I hope to stay in touch with after the war. I even met another chaplain to help me with the duties. We have our little adventures, of course. And I've seen too many wounded already. I do my job which is the Lord's work and feel proud to be in His service. But this has been kind of a light day for me, just sitting in my tent, smoking my pipe, and missing you two.

Hope to see you very soon.

Love, Emil."

She smiled, touched by her son's words, and asked, "Isn't that great?"

"It's amazing!" Enos replied.

Bessie glanced seriously at Enos and said, "Dinner might be late tonight. I have to read it a dozen more times." She rose from the table, taking her teacup in hand.

She laughed and walked off toward the living room, reading the letter to herself again as she went.

Enos watched her go, smiling. He thought about how great it was to see Bessie happy again and couldn't wait for the next letter to arrive. *Good job, son. You made your mother very happy today.* He stood up, whistling, and walked out of the house toward the barn, rolling up his sleeves and ready to get back to work.

Father Kapaun finished writing the letter and smiled. He thought it would please them. He was always careful not to tell them the gritty side of things for fear they'd worry even more. He slipped the letter into an envelope and addressed it to his beloved parents back in Pilsen, Kansas.

The rumbling of gunfire and explosions could still be heard in the far distance, but the noise seemed to be getting fainter. His pipe had gone out. He relit the pipe and went outside, gazing out over the terrain, thinking about how beautiful the surrounding area would be considered if the war would just end. He thought about why they were there and cursed the Communists once again. It was a beautiful country if only the Communists could leave it be.

A few days later resistance in the Kumchon pocket collapsed and it was time for the division to move north again.

Toward the front of the column, Sergeant Richardson kept glancing around, keenly searching for signs of the enemy from the passenger seat of his Jeep. Lieutenant Mike Dowe and Lieutenant Ralph Nardella sat in the back while Lieutenant Bob Wood drove.

The road cut through low verdant hills laced with lush rice paddies. Village huts continuously lined the road. The enemy could be inside or behind any or all of them, Richardson knew. Were they racing to encircle the North Koreans or were they headed into a trap?

"Where are we, Bill?" Lieutenant Nardella asked.

"About twenty miles south of Pyongyang," Richardson replied.

Lieutenant Nardella nodded in acknowledgment. "Good deal."

Suddenly, an enemy tank drove into view. The machine-gun sprayed the road with bullets. As the Americans in the convoy dove into the rice paddies to the side of the road, they saw three North Korean T-34/85s roar into life, defending from positions astride the main road into the next village. The lead tank moved forward. An American bazooka gunner ran out onto the road and fired at the lead tank. The rocket bounced off the tank with a thud, failing to detonate. A burst from the tank's turret machine-gun cut the brave gunner down.

Richardson yelled, "Ambush! Go for the treads!"

Lieutenant Nardella jumped out of the Jeep and ran up onto the road to grab the bazooka. With it in one hand, he turned and ran, dodging more incoming fire, to where the dead gunner's ammo box lay. Resting the launcher on the ground, he quickly slid a round partway into it, removed the arming pin, pushed the round fully in until it was latched in place, attached the wires from the back of the round to the contact spring, and hoisted it onto his shoulder. Seeing that the tank had moved closer and had exposed its side profile, he steadied himself and fired. The round exploded just above the tank's wheels. Nardella staggered back. The tank started to move again but the broken track rolled off the wheels, disabling it. Yet the crew did not bail. The tank's turret still worked, and it swiveled, firing wildly at the front of the now scattered convoy and the many GIs seeking cover.

Nardella loaded and fired another round, this time hitting the disabled tank towards its rear, scoring a hit on the engine, which promptly caught fire in a fury of flames, knocking the tank out of action and causing its crew to bail out. As they emerged from their hatches, they were caught in a vengeful hail of bullets from the nearby GIs. The two rear T-34/85s panicked, turned around awkwardly, and headed away, rolling into the village.

"Nice job, Lieutenant!" Sergeant Richardson yelled, his fist in the air.

"Thanks," Lieutenant Nardella responded. He rubbed his shoulder.

A pair of American M4A3E8 Sherman tanks rushed forward along the road, stopped next to the burning North Korean tank, and blasted the two retreating North Korean tanks, hitting their weaker rear armor and blowing them up.

By late afternoon, the earlier small ambush had developed into a full-blown battle. More enemy troops had been brought forward to reinforce the original ambush force. The villagers had all fled in terror. Mortar rounds were being fired from both armies near the village the T-34/85s had emerged from, identified by Richardson as Sariwon. Gunfire and explosions could be heard in the village ahead. Sergeant Richardson watched carefully as enemy soldiers began creeping through the brush readying for an assault on the American position. The American tanks' machine guns and the company's men poured a hail of fire on them, killing many of the enemy. The remaining North Korean soldiers turned tail and retreated, disappearing as if they'd never been there. Richardson shook his head in disbelief. The enemy was slippery while, he felt, the Americans sometimes seemed to stumble into things.

Medics attended to the many wounded American soldiers in the field. Father Kapaun administered aid to the closest wounded, performing last rites for those who didn't look like they were going to make it back to a field hospital.

A Dodge WC54 ambulance, clearly identified as such by the large red cross emblems painted on its sides, roof, and rear door, leaving the battlefield was the victim of a barrage of machine-gun fire, which hit the ambulance driver in the head, arm, and chest. The ambulance careened out of control before coming to a stop at the side of the road. The Communists had no respect for the wounded or the Rules of War, Kapaun thought. He rushed to the ambulance, jumped in, pushed the deceased driver aside, and took control as the enemy machine gunner continued to fire on the stricken ambulance. Father Kapaun drove it swiftly and erratically to the rear of the column before climbing out and checking on the men inside. He yelled to a nearby PFC to jump in the driver's seat. He was grateful to see that all of the men had miraculously escaped further injury from the incoming fire, and he gave thanks to God.

Lieutenant Bob Wood's squad took out the enemy machine position by executing a textbook squad-level attack. Yet the incoming mortar rounds continued to plague the American troops as they worked to establish better defensive positions. Meanwhile, it seemed that the remaining enemy soldiers had broken off contact and retreated as best they could.

Father Kapaun ran forward toward the front of the convoy where Sergeant Richardson was as he directed the deployment of the infantrymen.

"Father, it's still pretty hot here, so take to the ditch and keep low," Sergeant Richardson warned.

"I'm fine, Bill," Father Kapaun said. He smiled and lit his pipe.

A rifle shot came from nowhere, ripping Father Kapaun's pipe out of his hand. Sergeant Richardson spun around and took out the shooter, one of the previously injured North Koreans. Seemingly unfazed, Father Kapaun leaned down and retrieved the pipe. He took the precaution of bending low, but he pulled a roll of adhesive tape from his pocket and began mending the pipe once again.

"Most people worry about getting their head shot off. I think you worry more about that damned pipe," Sergeant Richardson said looking slightly aggrieved.

"Doesn't matter. Either way, this tape will fix anything," Father Kapaun responded.

Sergeant Richardson shook his head. "Great, now all I can visualize is you walking around giving last rites with your head held on by adhesive tape."

They laughed briefly. Sergeant Richardson looked at the pipe. It looked as good as new again. He thought, *If only I could fix up my men and these vehicles as easily as he fixes that pipe.*

Two days later, on October 19, the North Korean capital, Pyongyang, was taken by the US and ROK armies in a combined operation. A rumor spread among the men that this meant the war was over.

Chapter 7

October 20, 1950

Pyongyang

The night sky was quiet for a change outside the 3rd Battalion's new headquarters in Pyongyang, the North Korean capital. It was a large building in a dusty area where the wind was known to whip through, but the building itself was solid and well-guarded, giving the American staff officers the privacy they needed to plan their next moves.

The headquarters complex included a sizable hall where hundreds of soldiers attended a lavish event with plenty of food and drink to go around. The Army was treating them, and no one was turning that down.

Captain Shadish stood in front of a microphone on a small platform stage and cleared his throat. "Let me have your attention, everyone," Captain Shadish said, signaling Kapaun to come and join him on the stage.

Father Kapaun looked somewhat confused but reluctantly walked up to join Captain Shadish onstage, feeling out of his element. Everyone stopped talking and they turned around, giving their complete attention to Captain Shadish.

"I am pleased to honor one of our own tonight. By command of Major General Hobart R. Gay, Captain Emil J. Kapaun is hereby awarded the Bronze Star with V device for his display of heroism in action against the enemy near Kumchon, Korea, on October 13th, 1950," Captain Shadish announced.

Father Kapaun's eyes grew wide, and he blushed.

Everyone watched, smiling, as Captain Shadish presented the medal to a humbled Father Kapaun and saluted him. Father Kapaun saluted back, gingerly holding the medal in his hands as if he couldn't quite believe it was real.

"Congratulations, Father," Captain Shadish said.

Everyone in the place cheered and applauded.

"Thank you, Captain Shadish. Thank you," Father Kapaun said, smiling.

Still feeling a little uncomfortable, Father Kapaun quickly left the stage as the applause and cheers got louder and louder.

To one side of the hall, Doc Anderson, Sergeant Pappy Miller, Lieutenant Mike Dowe, and Lieutenant Ralph Nardella stood together, eating some of the food laid out on a sumptuous buffet. Lieutenant Bill Funchess stood nearby, grabbing his fair share of food, fearing it wouldn't last. Sergeant Vincent Doyle nearly knocked into Lieutenant Funchess as the pair went for some of the baked ham, and they both laughed.

"Sorry. Starving," Doyle said.

"No problem. Sergeant," Funchess said.

Sergeant Doyle continued to put food on his plate with one hand while reaching over and shaking Lieutenant Funchess' hand with his free hand.

"Vincent Doyle. Been here long?"

"Been in so many places it's hard to remember sometimes," Funchess replied jovially.

"I hear that. We've been chewing up some dirt ourselves," Vincent said, moving to collect still more food.

Lieutenant Nardella and Doc Anderson stood nearby talking.

"Father looked a little uncomfortable up there," Lieutenant Nardella commented.

"Come on, give him a break, Ralph. When you live your life doing things for others, the last thing you want is to have the spotlight on yourself," Doc said.

"Doc should know, right, guys?" Sergeant Miller chimed in.

They all laughed.

"All right, Pappy. Get out of here," Doc said, trying not to smile.

Lieutenant Bob Wood ran into the room looking downright gleeful with a spring in his step.

Doc noticed Wood's expression and did a double-take. He stared at Lieutenant Wood and said, "Bob, what the hell? Did the war just end or something?"

"I wish. But it's almost that good," Wood said, unable to wipe the smile from his face.

All eyes were on Bob as they waited. A few seconds went by and Doc said, "Are you going to tell us, or do we have to beat it out of you?"

Wood laughed, realizing everyone was waiting to hear the news.

"Oh, sorry. You'll never believe who just landed in Pyongyang!" Wood started.

"It's too early for Santa. Who?" Doc asked.

"Bob Hope!" Wood shouted.

"How's that almost as good as the war ending?" Lieutenant Nardella asked.

"I don't know. I love Bob Hope though. He always makes me laugh," Wood replied.

"Can't argue with that logic," Doc said.

☆ ☆ ☆

The next night, all four nurses hung out in the bathroom in their new living quarters in Pyongyang. These accommodations were considerably larger than their last place. The bathroom alone was about half the size of their previous sleeping quarters.

Mary and Deborah took showers in a large shower stall that had two shower faucets. Eva put on make-up by the sink while Sally washed her face.

"I can't believe we're seeing Bob Hope tonight," Mary said.

"Yeah, but why come all the way out here in the middle of a war?" Eva asked.

Sally sounded irritated when she said, "To make people laugh. Obviously."

Mary and Deborah looked at each other, both wincing at the way Sally responded.

"Yeah, I guess that makes sense," Eva said quietly.

They were all silent for a few moments. Then Sally said, "So, Deb, you have a date tonight?"

Mary and Deborah looked at each other; with Walt's death being so recent, dating seemed like a touchy subject. After a few moments, Deborah offered, "You could call it a date, I guess."

"Joe Ramirez, right?" Eva asked.

"Yeah," Deborah replied, feeling like maybe it was okay to talk about it after all, trying not to smile too broadly.

Mary noticed the smile and began to feel more comfortable as well. "He's cute," she said.

"Downright dreamy, if you ask me," Eva added.

"He'll do in a pinch," Deborah said.

"Don't make me pinch you," Mary teased.

Mary and Deborah laughed.

"Well, have a good time tonight," Sally said.

"Aren't you going, Sally?" Mary asked.

"I don't know. Haven't really decided yet," Sally replied.

"You really should go. Everyone needs a laugh," Deborah called out. She had shampoo in her eyes and didn't see that Sally had quietly left the room.

"She left," Eva informed Mary and Deborah.

"Damn, that was a little uncomfortable so soon after Walt dying," Deborah said.

"Sally might be better off not going," Mary said.

Mary turned off her water, wrapped a towel around herself, and stepped out of the shower.

"You might be right," Eva said.

Following suit, Deborah exited her shower. "Well, I'm going to have fun tonight. Even if it kills me."

Deborah thought about it for a second and added, "Did that sound harsh?"

"You deserve to have a good time, Deb," Mary said.

Mary began putting on make-up. Deborah smiled and said, "I do. Don't I?"

"Absolutely," Mary said.

Deborah began putting on make-up as the three women crowded around the large mirror making themselves look good for the event.

That night, with short notice and lots of security guarding the camp's perimeter, Bob Hope stood on stage at the Pyongyang airfield in front of a large crowd of excited soldiers and nurses, hoping that he'd be helping the entire audience to forget, for just a few moments, the awful place they were in and what was expected of them.

Many of the GIs wore their ceremonial yellow cavalry scarves but were dressed in their more casual field dress uniforms. Lieutenant Bob Wood sat up front, close to the improvised stage. Just behind him, Lieutenant Bill Funchess sat with Sergeant Vincent Doyle.

Bob Hope looked out at the crowd and, speaking into the microphone, said, "You know, every comedian has his own particular way of telling a joke. I tell 'em fast, Ed Wynn tells 'em slow, and Milton Berle tells 'em a week later ..."

The crowd exploded with laughter. Wood laughed so hard; he practically fell off the bench. Funchess and Doyle laughed, too, but they were laughing just as much at Bob Wood as Bob Hope.

"I wasn't sure television was here to stay, so I bought a very small set. It has a three-inch screen. You don't sit in front of it, you strap it over one eye," Bob Hope said.

The crowd laughed even harder as they all enjoyed the distraction from the grind of war and the comical genius of Bob Hope.

Deborah sat with Joe Ramirez, who was smiling like a kid with a new bicycle for Christmas. He put his arm around her nonchalantly. She smiled to herself. Then she leaned closer to him.

"I don't know how Truman and MacArthur feel about each other, but one left the Waldorf just as the other one entered. That was three days ago, and the revolving door is still spinning," Bob Hope said.

The crowd roared with laughter. It was laughter borne of relief and fear and anxiety all rolled up.

Sally sat off by herself and listened as Bob Hope told another twenty jokes or so. She heard the crowd laugh harder and harder at each one. After a while, Sally found herself smiling and even laughing at a few of the gags, able to breathe a little easier than before, and more than glad she'd made the tough decision to attend. She found herself wishing that Walt was there to share the laughter, but she pushed down her sadness and made a small prayer that he was safe in heaven.

Mary glanced at Lieutenant Mike Dowe, gave him a quick smile, then turned her head forward again.

"The difference between fighting the enemy and fighting with your wife is you'll only win one of those battles," Bob Hope said.

The crowd giggled.

"Sounds like you know which one," Bob Hope added.

The crowd went crazy with laughter.

Dowe took an empty seat next to Mary. "Hi, Mary. You look great tonight! Well, you always look great."

Mary smiled, blushing a little.

"Thank you. You don't look so bad yourself, Mike," Mary replied.

"Okay if I sit here?" Dowe asked.

"It's a free country. Well, back home it is anyway," Mary replied, playfully.

They smiled at each other and laughed.

"That was good. You could be the next Bob Hope," Dowe said.

"You think I look like a Bob?" Mary said, pretending to be insulted.

Dowe was clearly taken aback by Mary's admonishment and stammered, "No … I, I meant …"

Mary interrupted him with laughter and said, "Lighten up, Mike. It was just a joke."

Dowe recovered and laughed along with her, a big smile on his face.

Mary looked back at the stage, watching the show. But Dowe couldn't take his eyes off her.

He continued to look at her until she turned back toward him and smiled an inviting smile; he felt that he might have melted right there and then. He cautiously put his arm around her.

"I want to thank everyone for coming out tonight. Thank you for your service. God bless you. Goodnight," Bob Hope said, finishing his act.

Cheers and applause rang out. Hope walked to the front of the stage and shook the hands of a few soldiers; then he walked off stage, waving as he went.

☆ ☆ ☆

In a ramshackle hut near the stage area, Father Kapaun, choosing to skip the show, wrote a letter using ammo crates for an improvised desk. The show was just a sound in the distance, like the distant explosions and rattle of machinery he heard all the time. It was cold enough that he could see his breath, yet he didn't seem to mind. It reminded him of fishing with his father after a winter snowfall back on the farm.

"Dear Mr. and Mrs. Ward, with these few lines I wish to express to you my sympathy and sorrow for the loss of your son, John, killed in battle. John was a great man. I knew him personally and admired him very much. He fought very bravely, taking out many of the enemy soldiers who attacked our camp before losing his life. He will always be remembered as a hero."

He held the letter up to the lamplight and nodded his head. It was little enough but it would have to do.

On the makeshift desk was a stack of cards. Each held the name of a man who had been killed in action. On each card was the address of the next of kin and a notation as to whether he had administered the last rites.

Father Kapaun looked at the stack of cards, shaking his head. There were just so many of them. He stuffed the letter into an already addressed envelope, sealed it, picked up the card on top of the stack, and began writing the next condolence letter. It was the least he could do to honor those brave men and the loved ones left behind. He hoped the rumors were true and this was the last batch he would have to write.

☆ ☆ ☆

A few days later, the regiment was on the move again as huge convoys of U.S. Army jeeps, trucks, tanks, and artillery pieces traveled northward through rural North Korea. The soldiers were miserable, even though the war had decidedly turned in the favor of the United Nations forces. There was no telling what was going to happen next. They were all afraid of traveling into another ambush and disappointed that the war was not over after all. A GI dropped his yellow 8th Cavalry scarf out the back of a truck and the wind picked it up, quickly whisking it away into the inhospitable landscape.

General McArthur had said this was the final big push. That the war might still be over by Christmas. Communism would be driven from the Korean peninsula.

Supporting the 3rd Battalion for the next operation was a 155mm Howitzer Battery from the 99th Field Artillery, the 8th Engineer Battalion, three badass-looking Sherman tanks, a platoon of heavy mortars, medics, and others ready for anything, despite how they felt.

☆ ☆ ☆

It was Halloween, October 31, 1950, but this was no trick or treat for the Americans. Near the town of Unsan, North Korea, approximately fifty miles south of the Yalu River and the Chinese border, 600 GIs of the 3rd Battalion dug foxholes and an arc perimeter of connecting foxholes and bunkers about 400 yards in diameter.

On the mountaintops overlooking Unsan, observation posts were being hastily constructed by the supporting engineers. Behind them and below in the valley, the artillery battery set up its firing positions, digging emplacements for the guns and storage bunkers for their ammunition.

To the north of Unsan, the enemy burned numerous fires, which sent thick plumes of smoke in an attempt to conceal the columns of enemy troops who were quietly moving into the area.

☆ ☆ ☆

Sergeant Pappy Miller had been out on patrol with his section. He escorted an old Korean farmer through the outer security perimeter and towards the 3rd Battalion command post.

Inside, Captain Shadish and Master Sergeant Bill Richardson stood face to face, seemingly at odds with one another.

"Bill, you've gotta get these men out of the valley and onto higher ground. They're too vulnerable. There's no defense if you're hit!" Shadish said.

"With all due respect, Sir, these men know how to dig in and they know how to fight," Richardson replied, not wanting to argue with Shadish, a dear friend, but also not wanting to move the men who he felt were in the right place to defend the command post.

Shadish frowned and shook his head. "I hope they know how to die, too."

The Sergeant closed his eyes and nodded.

"Sorry, Captain. You're right. I'll move them right away," Richardson said.

"Thank you, Bill. You know I always value your opinion, but sometimes you just need to listen to me. Being on the low ground is never a good idea. Gives the enemy too much of an advantage."

"You're right, Sir. I'll get right on it."

Shadish nodded at Richardson and walked out of the tent.

Sergeant Richardson also left the tent and started walking in the direction of the front-line company command posts on the valley floor to move the men. He nearly collided with Sergeant Pappy Miller.

"Whaddya need, Pappy?" Sergeant Richardson asked, irritated.

"Bill, this man lives about three miles from here. He was shocked yesterday to find several Chinese soldiers passing through his farm," Pappy said.

Sergeant Richardson looked at the short, middle-aged man, confused, and said, "Sir, how do you know they were Chinese?"

"Padded brown uniforms. Remember them from last war," the old man replied. He spat on the ground.

Sergeant Richardson wasn't convinced. He said, "And how do I know you're not bullshitting us to try to get goodies for your family?"

"Want nothing. Chinese soldiers scare family. Seem not good," the farmer replied.

"I spoke with him for quite a while, Sergeant. He seems credible," Sergeant Miller added.

Sergeant Richardson sighed. "The Chinese. That's all we need." He glanced at the farmer, nodded, and said, "Thank you."

The farmer nodded back.

With that, Sergeant Richardson continued his walk to the front-line command posts intent on updating command and the individual company commanders on the developing situation.

Sergeant Miller smiled at the farmer. Then he went into the mess tent and came out with a couple cans of Spam. He handed them to the man who smiled his thanks and walked away. Miller hoped the farmer's word was enough to convince Sergeant Richardson to take certain actions, but he wasn't sure that it was.

☆ ☆ ☆

Before Sergeant Richardson could reach the first company commander's position, machine-guns from the nearby hills unleashed a crossfire of bullets around him, ricocheting in all directions.

The sergeant dove to the ground. Nurse Eva, nearby, also hit the ground, looking all around, fear in her face. Sergeant Vincent Doyle, Lieutenant Mike Dowe, and PFC Tibor Rubin began returning fire at the soldiers in brown padded uniforms who poured from the hills and into the valley. But it seemed like the more they killed, the more men appeared.

Mortar rounds exploded all around them. Richardson saw several American soldiers go down. He had no faith they were still alive.

Nurse Eva got up and began to run, screaming as she did so, trying to avoid the mortar blasts.

"Eva, stay down," Richardson yelled.

Before Eva could fall to the ground, she was gunned down. He heard her grunt and then heard her gasp for air.

Sergeant Richardson winced as he watched Eva, only a few feet away, riddled with bullets and bleeding heavily. He could hear the death rattle in her throat.

Sergeant Richardson looked over at his 'handie talkie' radio, wanting to call in more troops, but the radio had been smashed by an incoming bullet. Another explosion knocked him into a ditch. In desperation, he threw a grenade, taking out several enemy soldiers who were approaching from his right dressed in padded brown uniforms. They were definitely Chinese, just like the farmer had said.

Two Chinese soldiers ran forward firing submachine guns, killing several more American soldiers. Then they turned and dashed off, leaving a trail of several dead bodies behind. Richardson rose in defiance and anger, rifle at the ready. They were gone.

☆ ☆ ☆

Later that afternoon, Sergeant Richardson stood inside the battalion command post with Lieutenant Mike Dowe and Sergeant Pappy Miller. They watched Doc Anderson as he attended to the soldiers who still had a chance. They occasionally glanced over at Nurse Eva's dead body.

Father Kapaun stood at Eva's side, praying over her as Mary, Deborah, and Sally tearfully watched, shaking their heads. They had their arms around one another, and their bodies were shivering. Kapaun gently spoke in a soft voice, trying to comfort them.

"I wish we'd gotten that information about the Chinese troops earlier. We could've been better prepared," Sergeant Richardson said.

"Sorry. I got that farmer back here as fast as I could once I heard about it," Sergeant Miller said.

"It's not your fault, Pappy. Just bad timing," Sergeant Richardson said assuringly.

"We need to quit losing so many good men . . . and women, too, for that matter," Lieutenant Dowe said. His body was straight, and his hands were clenched by his sides.

"We need to stop losing anyone and take the battle to them," Sergeant Richardson replied.

"Do we even know what the Chinese plan on doing?" Lieutenant Dowe asked. He was tightly wound, his face a mask of anger and fear.

"Other than killing every one of us? Afraid not," Sergeant Richardson replied.

Doc looked at Richardson and said, "Bill, we need better defenses than this. They come in and do this another couple of times and I'm afraid we're done for."

Sergeant Richardson nodded at Doc. "I know. The Captain and I spoke about it earlier. I'm on it. And I'm so sorry about Eva, Doc."

"So am I, Bill. You have no idea," Doc said, shaking his head before going back to his work.

Bill looked at the soldiers around him and yelled, "You heard the Doc. Let's set up a defense to protect everyone. Now!"

They all ran from the command post as Bill hurried through the room, practically chasing them outside.

Chapter 8

October 31, 1950

Unsan

On the road to the south of Unsan, a convoy containing four deuce-and-a-half trucks, five Dodge ambulances, and an M24 Chaffee light tank assembled to evacuate the wounded. Nearly one hundred wounded soldiers lay on stretchers on the ground and in the vehicles while nearly twice as many walking wounded assembled nearby. It was a scene of near-total chaos as sporadic gunfire and mortar rounds struck indiscriminately. Several of the men returned fire in the direction of the enemy.

PFC Patrick Schuler parked his Jeep as Father Kapaun jumped out and ran over to the lead truck. Sergeant Burt Coer sat in the cab of the lead truck, talking on the radio. "Sir, I don't care if the 23rd Infantry followed orders. Did they make it out? I've got over a hundred wounded here, and I need permission to take them out on the same road."

Sergeant Coer listened for a moment, rolled his eyes, and asked, "Then what in the hell are we supposed to do with them?" He winced and held the radio away from his ear. All Father Kapaun could hear was loud static and Chinese chatter.

Father Kapaun stepped on the running board of the lead truck, looked hopeful, and asked, "What did he say?"

Sergeant Coer shook his head and replied, "He said it's every man for himself. Then the radio cut out."

"Do you have clearance to move out?"

"Not really."

"What're we supposed to do?" Kapaun asked in despair.

Sergeant Coer sighed and said, "They said to stay put, Father, but I think we can bust through with our tank. We can squeeze you and your wounded in somewhere."

Father Kapaun looked at the overcrowded convoy. Wounded men lay everywhere, far too many to be loaded onto the vehicles. He looked dubiously at the tank sat at the front of the convoy. The sergeant noticed and said, "It might not be a Sherman, but it can still shoot."

Father Kapaun nodded and stepped down. "Go ahead. I've got another forty or so men wounded at the command post, and I'm not leaving them behind."

"That post is going to be overrun, Father. Sure as shootin'," Sergeant Coer said.

"I'll do my best to protect them. What other choice do we have?" Father Kapaun said walking away.

"Suit yourself," the sergeant said.

Father Kapaun ran back to his Jeep; he and Schuler headed back to the command post. The convoy of wounded moved out despite many wounded soldiers remaining on the side of the road. Several men desperately jumped onto the outside of moving vehicles. Those who were too wounded to walk called out not to be left behind.

Coer shook his head and tried the radio again. Just more static.

The sun was beginning to set when Schuler parked the Jeep outside the command post, and Father Kapaun quickly got out. Doc Anderson was just exiting the tent.

"What happened with the evacuation convoy?" Doc asked.

"They moved out, but it's total chaos out there. Even if they had the room to carry more, I think the Chinese have us cut off," Father Kapaun replied.

They watched as illumination flares lit up the sky followed by machine-gun fire and mortar rounds exploding as both sides gave it everything they had.

☆ ☆ ☆

As the evacuation convoy made its way down the road south of Unsan, the Chinese hit the convoy hard from both sides of the road with assault rifles, machine-guns, and a Type 36 57mm recoilless rifle. The M24 tank and several vehicles were destroyed completely or on fire, the remainder were immobilized. The wounded men tried to find cover as best they could, but they were raked with machine-gun fire, which killed many of them. Those that got away shivered in the sparse cover. There was now no way to get to safety. The setting sun finally disappeared behind the mountains. It got colder, much colder.

☆ ☆ ☆

The next day, Wednesday, November 1, 1950, light snow flurries fell over the remnants of the 3rd Battalion, 8th Regiment, 1st Cavalry Division. Mortar rounds exploded sporadically from the surrounding hills which were covered in smoke. Harassing sniper fire spattered the area. The remaining U.S. soldiers dug trenches and prepared defenses as best they could, but the already desperate situation was looking grimmer with each passing moment. The cold was the least of their worries.

The bodies of more than 2,000 dead Chinese soldiers lay around the perimeter of the camp, and the general consensus was that soon there would be several thousands more coming for the Americans.

On the only road leading out to the south, what was left of the battalion's vehicles was lined up haphazardly behind the wreckage of the convoy that had been destroyed the prior evening. The men were preparing for another evacuation attempt even though they knew the road ahead was controlled by a Chinese blocking party.

Father Kapaun and Sergeant Bill Richardson looked around at the many dead and wounded soldiers from both armies.

"Do you know what day it is, Bill?" Father Kapaun asked.

"No idea, Father."

"It's All Saints' Day," Father Kapaun replied, lighting his pipe.

"We could use some help from above right about now," Bill said. He rubbed his eyes.

"That's for sure," Father Kapaun said.

A U.S. Sikorsky H-5 helicopter landed nearby amid fire from the hills. Father Kapaun dumped out the contents of his pipe, stashed the pipe in his shirt pocket, and rushed towards the helicopter to unload the much-needed supplies.

A warrant officer kicked the supplies out of the helicopter's side door as a sniper's rounds hit the chopper. Father Kapaun hit the ground. Lieutenant Bill Funchess popped up out of a foxhole and took out the sniper and two more Chinese soldiers positioned near the sniper.

Father Kapaun, seeing this, nodded at Funchess. The lieutenant nodded back before disappearing back into the relative safety of his foxhole.

Father Kapaun, loaded down with boxes of supplies, walked off. He marveled that he could be so calm in the face of such chaos. Yes, he'd been in the theatre of battle before, but it never got old. There was always something to look out for, to be wary of. To be afraid of.

Three thousand feet above the ongoing scenes of carnage, the observer of a U.S. AT-6 Texan 'forward air control' plane looked down and saw a mass of enemy troops one valley over from Unsan. He keyed the radio microphone and said, "My God, there are so many Chinese soldiers down there it looks like the entire hillside is covered with ants!"

After broadcasting its position, the AT-6 banked and turned around to head south; its crew was glad to have avoided any enemy fighter planes and happy to see some of their own, the ones they were spotting for in the distance. They approached and then passed beneath them.

Minutes later, as they entered the valley, the flight of six F-51D Mustang fighter bombers strafed Chinese columns with a hail of half-inch machine-gun fire, each plane in turn dropping its two 1000-pound bombs to devastating effect. After circling around, the Mustangs made a second pass through the valley, this time releasing their drop tanks which had been repurposed as inflammatory bombs. The napalm they contained erupted into massive fireballs, incinerating hundreds of Chinese soldiers. Their screams echoed throughout the valley. The smell of burning fuel and human flesh filled the air.

Lieutenant Dowe sat down before his platoon commander duties to write a quick letter home.

"Dear Dad:

I hope this letter finds you well. We are experiencing a lot of enemy fire, most of it from the Chinese. I can't tell you where we are; the Army would just redact it anyway. But it hasn't been pleasant. From what you and your friends—as reported by you—are saying, I would say Americans don't have a very good sense of this war. We've been told, of course, that we're fighting to keep Communism from coming to America. I don't know about that. I often believe we're fighting this war just to satisfy some bureaucrats in Washington who want to spend money and human flesh to make a point.

The North Koreans are vicious enough, but the Chinese are not only vicious, they're numerous. Some days, we see them pouring from the hills like ants at a picnic. It's all I can do to stand in one spot and fire without shitting my pants. We've lost so many men already and we've only been at this for three and a half months. It seems like years since I sat at the edge of the pond out back and fished. It seems like years since I've seen you.

We have a wonderful chaplain here who motivates us all to be more spiritual and, believe it or not, braver. He thinks nothing of walking upright onto the field of battle to give some soldier last rites or throwing a wounded man over his shoulder to carry him to safety. He's an inspiration to all of us. I wish you could meet him.

Well, I'm off back to taking care of my platoon.

I love you and miss you.

Mike"

On the battlefield south of Unsan, Father Kapaun approached Captain Shadish who was standing next to Lieutenant Mike Dowe. "Captain, I would like to perform a mass."

Captain Shadish's eyes widened, and he asked, "Now? With everything that's going on?"

"Captain, I feel like the men could use their spirits lifted. Besides, it is All Saints' Day," Father Kapaun responded.

Captain Shadish considered Kapaun's request for a moment and then nodded. "Well, in that case, go for it, Father. Just be careful you don't get your head shot off. Or anyone else's for that matter."

Father Kapaun smiled and nodded, saying, "I won't, sir. Thank you." Father Kapaun walked away to prepare himself.

Shadish turned to Lieutenant Dowe and said, "Nothing frightens that man, does it?"

Mike laughed and said, "I think you're right. He's a good man. I can't image how much harder things would be without him around to keep our spirits up, even in times like these."

"You're right about that," Shadish agreed. If this was part of the plan to get him out of the war safely, he was for it.

The captain nodded and watched as Father Kapaun removed his helmet, gathered his Mass items, and donned his purple stole. To the captain, he looked like an exotic bird out of place in this dismal war.

PFC Schuler, his leg bandaged and walking stiffly, helped Father Kapaun set up an altar on the hood of a Jeep while several GIs approached with curiosity despite the increased sniper fire.

"Thank you, Patrick," Father Kapaun said.

"You're welcome, Father," Schuler replied.

Captain Shadish, Lieutenant Mike Dowe, Sergeant Bill Richardson, Nurse Mary, PFC Tibor Rubin, Doc Anderson, Sergeant Pappy Miller, Lieutenant Bill Funchess, Nurse Deborah, PFC Joe Ramirez, Lieutenant Bob Wood, Sergeant Vincent Doyle, PFC Peter Busatti, Lieutenant Ralph Nardella, and Nurse Sally all stood in front of a crowd of people, waiting for Father Kapaun to say mass.

Father Kapaun saw a huddle of GIs whom he did not know standing nearby and said to one, "Why don't you join us, soldier?"

"Some of us aren't even Catholic, Father," one of the GIs replied.

"Come anyway. Pray in your own way. What's important is your faith," Father Kapaun said. He motioned with his arm for them to join.

The GI nodded his head and said, "Okay." As he moved forward, many of the others joined him as well.

Father Kapaun lifted his hands and said to the crowd, "Lord, hear our prayers." Then he began delivering an abbreviated mass.

With mortar rounds exploding less than two hundred yards away, Father Kapaun never once flinched. He was deeply devoted to his work and God was more important than the chaos around him. Other men watched from a distance, from tanks, from the guard posts, all over the place. The men were so influenced by his courage that no one moved until the mass was over.

The crowd broke up and everyone immediately rushed back to their duty stations. Doc Anderson and Nurse Mary walked quickly towards the aid station.

"Father Kapaun seems to have more lives than a herd of cats," Doc said.

"More guts, too," Mary added.

They laughed lightly and continued walking towards the aid tent.

Deborah and Sally followed some twenty feet behind. Sally looked horrified. Deborah noticed and asked, "What's wrong, Sally?"

"I don't know. I just have a bad feeling in the pit of my stomach," Sally responded.

"In that case, let's get inside fast. I don't want to be out here if all hell is about to break loose," Deborah replied.

They hurried their pace, caught up to Doc and Mary, and made their way into the aid station tent while Doc held the door open for them.

Inside the command post, Lieutenant Mike Dowe, looking defeated, stood with the radio mic in his hand. Lieutenant Bill Funchess walked up to him. "You just get some bad news, Mike?"

"Is it that obvious?" Dowe asked.

Funchess nodded, waiting for him to elaborate.

"I just heard the Chinese have us blocked in. We've got orders to escape under the cover of darkness," Dowe said.

"I thought the 5th Calvary was coming to help," Lieutenant Funchess said, looking spooked.

Lieutenant Dowe shook his head. "We are the calvary now. Tell your men to get 'MAD' at those Chinese sons-of-bitches. Anger overpowers fear every time."

☆ ☆ ☆

The nurses sat quietly inside their tent. Explosions could still be heard in the distance and they all looked and felt nervous.

Mary looked at Eva's bed and said, "I can't believe Eva's gone."

Deborah nodded and said, "Neither can I. It feels so wrong. None of us are safe anymore."

"We never were safe," Mary added.

Sally sighed and said, "So true. I feel great about all of the soldiers I've helped. Doc is amazing but as great as he is he couldn't have done this without our help. I just want this war to end and to be able to go back home and live my life. You know? Meet a guy, get married, raise a family. That sort of thing rather than walking around a camp that could get bombed at any moment."

Mary nodded. "And it's only been four months." Deborah seemed even more frightened than before.

"Why don't we go back to work?" Deborah said.

"Yeah, I think I'd feel safer there around other people myself," Mary agreed.

They all nodded and left the tent, each woman looking back at Eva's bed as she left.

Chapter 9

South of Unsan, The Night

of November 1st, 1950

Mortar and rocket fire hit the 3rd Battalion perimeter as flares in the night sky revealed thousands of Chinese soldiers streaming into the valley from the hills on both sides. Father Kapaun and Doc Anderson were outside the aid station having just loaded two of the wounded soldiers onto a Jeep.

"I don't think we're going to be able to get them all out, Father," Doc said. He was weary and scared. Though it was his duty as a doctor to care for these men, he felt helpless to carry on.

"Well, we can't just leave them," Father Kapaun said. He briskly turned to go back inside.

Sergeant Pappy Miller ran over, panicked, yelling, "They're everywhere! They're everywhere! We need to go!"

Doc thought about it a second, nodded, and said, "He's right. There are just too many of them. Too many soldiers. Too many wounded."

Father Kapaun shook his head. "I can't leave. God gave me this work."

Doc, exasperated, said, "Is God going to keep us from being killed?"

Kapaun paused and put his hand on Doc's shoulder. "God's will may be unknown to us, but His will is to help these men."

Sergeant Miller, frustrated, ran off towards his squad's machine-gun pit as Father Kapaun hoisted another wounded man onto his shoulder to load into the Jeep.

Sergeant Vincent Doyle ran towards them, screaming, "Father Kapaun!"

Father Kapaun turned and stared at Sergeant Doyle who was pointing towards the fields.

Hundreds more Chinese soldiers ran towards them, coming down the hills and fanning out across the plains. Red tracer rounds from Chinese machine-guns flashed across the area. Orange tracer rounds replied, headed in the opposite direction fired back from the M1919 Browning .30 caliber machine-gun teams, commanded by Sergeant Pappy Miller, Lieutenant Ralph Nardella, and several other NCOs and junior officers. The noise and stench emitted from the machine-guns were incredible. The ammonia emitted from the massive number of rounds being fired caused the soldiers' eyes to water and noses to run, adding to the already dark situation.

PFC Patrick Schuler saw the Chinese breaking through the perimeter immediately in front of him as bullets rained down all over. Seeing no alternative, Schuler set the disabled Jeep he'd been using as cover on fire with a thermite grenade before fleeing towards the rear with others. As he was running, he saw an artillery round explode near the command post, leaving a white cloud behind. Desiring some cover, he ran towards the command post. But then he realized that the dreaded white phosphorous incendiary round had been thrown into the mix of incoming Chinese shells; this mix burned everything it touched, including metal, clothing, human flesh. It was impossible to extinguish. Schuler ran changed course, heading towards the mess station.

Stragglers from other units in the area that had been further forward filtered into the command post's perimeter. It was complete and utter chaos. Morale had started to break down as the casualties mounted. Ammunition levels were dropping fast, and it was getting colder, much colder.

"Where are Pappy and Vincent?" Sergeant Richardson asked Lieutenant Dowe as they stood in a corner of the command post.

"I don't know where anyone is," Lieutenant Dowe responded, running his fingers through his hair.

Sergeant Richardson looked pissed, yelling out, "Damn. We need to hightail it out of here while we still have a chance. And Lieutenant, you might want to remove your collar insignia. The Chinese snipers are trained to take out our officers first."

Lieutenant Dowe's eyes bulged. He nodded, ripping off his insignias. Hearing this, all other officers in the room followed suit and removed their insignias as well.

☆ ☆ ☆

Outside, on the front line of the battalion command post's inner security perimeter, Sergeant Pappy Miller saw an enemy soldier's head pop up. He crawled out of his machine-gun fire pit to get a bit closer and lobbed a grenade at the soldier. His grenade landed inside the occupied shell-hole and exploded, taking the soldier out.

Thinking he had neutralized the immediate risk to his squad, Sergeant Miller crawled back towards the relative safety of the machine-gun pit, not seeing the grenade another enemy soldier had tossed in his direction landing just behind him. The grenade exploded. The blast and several shrapnel fragments severely wounded Sergeant Miller's left leg.

Sergeant Miller covered his mouth to stop himself from screaming and giving his position away. He looked around, feeling as if he was about to die. In excruciating pain, he faced the command post and yelled, "Medic! Medic!"

But no one heard anything amidst the cacophony of battle.

Over in the field to the west of the command post and aid station, the attached platoon of Sherman tanks fired away, killing dozens of Chinese soldiers at a time. Yet it made no difference. More soldiers filled in, stepping over their dead comrades and moving toward the Americans.

Another white phosphorus round exploded near the command post's defensive perimeter. A GI screamed, his body burning from the metal shards. Father Kapaun ran to the man and tried to pat him down, but he had to let go when he felt his own hands burning. As he managed to dislodge the phosphorus fragments from his own hands, for the first time he felt truly helpless and the burning, screaming soldier expired before his eyes.

PFC Tibor Rubin fired away with his smoking machine-gun, dropping Chinese soldiers by the dozens, yet they kept coming. He felt a thud behind him and turned to see Sergeant Richardson with an ammunition box.

Rubin yelled, "Sarg, I can't see a thing!"

"Light up the trucks! Put these tracer rounds on the trucks!" Bill ordered, screaming at the top of his lungs as he opened the box and pulled out a 50-round ammo belt.

PFC Rubin took the end of the belt and feed it into the left side of the M1919 Browning .30 caliber machine-gun. Pulling the cocking handle back and releasing, he turned the machine-gun toward the trucks and began firing. The tracer rounds ignited the canvas tops and fuel tanks of the trucks. Huge explosions rocked the area.

Sergeant Richardson left Rubin's machine-gun pit and ran to where Lieutenant Dowe, a calmed down PFC Schuler, and Sergeant

Doyle had set up a position from which they were firing rifle grenades at the Chinese on the other side of the perimeter wire. Several of the trucks around them had been set on fire and were randomly exploding. The whole area was lit up.

Back in his pit, PFC Rubin's eyes grew wide. In front of him, hordes of Chinese soldiers descended. They looked like southern fire ants streaming out of an anthill. The ones in front fired their submachine guns. PFC Rubin swung the machine-gun around and resumed firing, taking out several of the enemy as they ran toward the command post. He knew he risked friendly casualties, but he had to stop the Chinese from breaking through.

PFCs Joe Ramirez and Peter Busatti were in Lieutenant Ralph Nardella's machine-gun pit engaging wave after wave of assaulting Chinese. The bodies were piling up like a dam in front of their eyes. Lieutenants Bill Funchess and Bob Wood were stunned by the sight before them, yet they continued firing away, shooting the onrushing Chinese like fish in a barrel. The enemy didn't spread out or take evasive action. They just kept streaming toward the American position.

Grenades were lobbed back and forth. Mortar rounds exploded all over the place. Soldiers on both sides were screaming and dying, some even hit by friendly fire in the increasing chaos.

The injured Sergeant Miller crawled as best he could, blood pouring from his now useless leg as he tried to make his way back to the relative safety of the command post.

Nurse Sally emerged from the aid station and stood just outside the command post looking around for people she could help when she noticed Sergeant Miller and her eyes grew wide. She glanced around quickly, trying to get someone's attention to go after Sergeant Miller, but everyone was too busy to notice her pleas for assistance. Seeing how much pain Sergeant Miller was in, she rushed forward to try to help him alone.

It looked like the advancing Chinese were starting to get beaten back when yet another wave charged in from the east, killing numerous fatigued American soldiers as they advanced.

Father Kapaun continued to run from foxhole to foxhole, dragging the wounded to cover, saying prayers over the dying and hearing confessions whilst hails of bullets ripped up the earth around him, yet he was undaunted and untouched. Father Kapaun jumped into a foxhole next to PFC Peter Busatti who had been on his way to retrieve more ammo for Lieutenant Nardella's machine-gun.

"Peter, are you hurt?" Father Kapaun asked.

PFC Busatti pulled his shirt up to show Father Kapaun a bleeding shrapnel wound on the left side of his back. Father Kapaun nodded and began applying peroxide to the wound and pulled his last field dressing from his pocket. With the dressing applied, PFC Busatti continued on his way to grab more ammo for the machine-gun.

Nurse Sally reached Sergeant Miller and leaned down, trying to assess his wounds, and realized they were even worse than she originally thought.

"Can you walk?" Nurse Sally asked, already sure she knew the answer.

Sergeant Miller shook his head. He was now in too much pain to speak.

He pointed to his left leg. She nodded, knowing there was no way he could walk out of there by himself, and said, "Come on, let's get you to safety."

Sergeant Miller nodded. Nurse Sally got him to his feet and took a few steps, supporting him with her right shoulder. She always liked Sergeant Miller and was happy to help him, proud to be the only one noticing him down and able to get him back to the aid station. After a couple of steps, she saw a Chinese soldier step out from behind a tree stump some twenty yards away and aim his submachine gun in their direction. Before she could react, he fired several rounds, one hitting her in the left shoulder, causing her to spin around to her left and fall to the ground; a second bullet hit her in the chest and a third her head, before she hit the ground, landing on her back. The enemy soldier continued to fire.

Sergeant Miller lost his balance and fell heavily to the ground. He lay still with his head facing Sally's, playing possum. The Chinese soldier moved back to a safe position behind the tree trunk. Sergeant Miller tried not to move although his view of Sally dying, blood pouring from her head, was heartbreaking. She began to gag on her own blood and within seconds, she died. Sergeant Miller had no choice but to lie without moving, trying not to attract the Chinese soldier's attention, but he couldn't hold back the tears as he looked at Sally who'd so bravely given her life in an attempt to save his.

Sergeants Richardson and Doyle found themselves kneeling side by side, near Lieutenant Dowe's machine-gun pit, firing whilst the machine-gun team loaded yet another belt of ammo. Doyle looked over and saw Father Kapaun crouched over, running a football field's length out to retrieve yet another wounded GI. He was missing his helmet.

Sergeant Doyle yelled at Richardson, "Bill, tell Kapaun to get his ass back here!"

Sergeant Richardson looked over and saw Father Kapaun selflessly trying to rescue the wounded GI and said, barely under his breath, "Dammit." He scrambled a few feet away, cupped his hand around his mouth, and yelled towards Father Kapaun, "Father, get your ass back here now!"

The sergeants watched Father Kapaun run on; suddenly, he stopped. Thinking the chaplain was finally listening to them, they nodded and briefly smiled at each other. They looked back at Father Kapaun and saw that he now had his hands raised in the air, surrounded by four Chinese soldiers who had leaped out of a nearby trench.

The sergeants ducked, pissed. Several GIs heads looked out from their foxholes. One of them shouted, "They got Father Kapaun!"

"I can't believe it," Lieutenant Dowe said.

"We're all screwed now," PFC Ramirez said, despondently shaking his head.

"Like hell!" Lieutenant Dowe yelled, committed to turning things around. He looked at Sergeant Richardson and they nodded at each other.

The Chinese soldiers began leading Father Kapaun away.

Lieutenant Mike Dowe, PFC Joe Ramirez, PFC Tibor Rubin, PFC Patrick Schuler, and Lieutenant Bill Funchess all shot, taking down all four of the Chinese soldiers, leaving Kapaun standing alone.

Father Kapaun looked around, stunned. Unharmed, he ran back to the relative safety of a nearby squad's fire position, keeping lower to the ground than usual. That had been close. He said a prayer of thanks.

Sergeant Miller continued to crawl, looking back at Nurse Sally with a heavy heart. He inched his way closer to the battalion command post. He rolled into a ditch, his left ankle and calf badly wounded from the grenade.

As a Chinese soldier approached, crouching trying to avoid detection, Sergeant Miller lobbed a grenade at him. The enemy soldier flew through the air from the force of the blast, his body falling stone dead. Sergeant Miller checked his belt only to discover he was out of grenades. "Damn. What do I do now?"

Nearby, another Chinese soldier maneuvered towards Sergeant Miller, looking at all of the other dead American soldiers on the ground. He looked down at one, saw him breathing, shot him in the head, and moved on, getting closer to Sergeant Miller.

Sergeant Miller grabbed the body of another dead G.I. and pulled the body over him, hiding himself as best he could.

☆ ☆ ☆

The level of small arms fire around the command post had escalated. Inside the command post, the officers were trying to secure more artillery and air support missions to soak up more of the enemy forces. With the aid station overflowing, many of the wounded were now housed in the command post. The number of soldiers still in good fighting shape was dwindling fast and some of the wounded were given weapons to defend the command post.

Doc Anderson worked on a soldier who had been shot several times as Nurses Mary and Deborah applied pressure to the larger wound. But the man was worse off than they had hoped, and he went into cardiac arrest, dying on the table before they could stabilize him.

"Dammit. I'm tired of this shit," Doc said, his face turning red with anger and frustration. He threw down his instruments.

The nurses looked sympathetically at Doc. They bit their lips to stop themselves from saying something they desperately wanted to say but knew they shouldn't.

Suddenly a Chinese soldier jumped through the window behind them, a grenade in his hand. He pulled the pin. Doc grabbed an M1 carbine lying on the table next to him, shot the Chinese soldier in the head, and screamed, "Duck!" as he fell to the ground.

Everyone else hit the ground as quickly as possible. The Chinese soldier fell backward through the window, dropping the grenade outside. Three seconds later the grenade went off, blowing the dead soldier back into the command post and taking out a portion of the back wall.

Doc threw the carbine down, turned and looked at the nurses, and said, "Bring me the next one, Mary."

"Maybe you should take a break," Mary suggested.

"I don't have time to take a break," Doc replied.

Deborah walked around to Doc, gently touched his face, and said, "Mary's right. Have a seat and rest for a few minutes. You need it."

Doc nodded. He sat and covered his face with his bloody hands. Mary and Deborah exchanged half-smiles, knowing someone needed to convince Doc to take a break before he had a nervous breakdown and lost his sanity. He'd be no use to anyone then.

A few moments later a Chinese officer, Captain Yi, staggered into the command post, severely wounded. Everyone looked around, not knowing what to do. Captain Yi yelled in perfect English, "Don't shoot. Help me!" before he collapsed, landing on the floor already occupied by the many American wounded.

Father Kapaun came through the door and went to the wounded Chinese officer, hesitating as he looked at his uniform. Then he began to bandage the officer's wounds. Nurses Mary and Deborah watched, astounded.

☆ ☆ ☆

Later that night in the aid station, Father Kapaun continued to work tirelessly, attending to and blessing the wounded soldiers and praying over the deceased. The nurses came by, looking for a place to sleep. They stopped to watch Father Kapaun for a moment, touched by his dedication. They looked at each other.

Father Kapaun turned, nodded at them, and said, "Ladies? Can't sleep?"

"We're tired enough," Mary said, yawning.

"Yeah, you can say that again," Deborah added, rubbing her eyes.

"Just ... finding a spot where we could even lay our heads down is not an easy task," Nurse Mary said. She wasn't even sure she could sleep with the constant noises of the battle and the injured men.

They looked around. A few soldiers on guard duty paced around near the entrance, but the majority of people were either sleeping or dead. All the beds were filled with wounded soldiers. Father Kapaun made a face and added, "It doesn't smell so good here, either."

Mary and Deborah shook their heads in despair.

Father Kapaun smiled and said, "Of course, there's always the jail."

The nurses looked confused.

"Jail?" Mary asked, wondering if she heard him correctly.

"Just a small room with bars on it over on the far side. It is empty as far as I know," Father Kapaun said.

"Empty? Seriously?" Deborah asked.

"I think so," Father Kapaun replied.

Mary and Deborah looked at each other, nodding their heads. Nurse Mary said, "Let's go check it out before anyone else thinks of it."

"Okay," Deborah said, looking slightly pleased.

"Thanks, Father," Mary said.

"Yes, thanks, Father," Deborah added.

"Any time. Goodnight, ladies. Get some sleep. You need it," Father Kapaun said.

"You get some sleep, too, Father," Deborah suggested.

"Plenty of time for me to sleep when I'm dead," Father Kapaun responded, smiling as he went back to work.

☆ ☆ ☆

The nurses, completely exhausted, arrived at the jail cell. Deborah opened the cell door. As Father Kapaun had promised, it was empty. Inside there were two small cots in it that had seen better days.

"Might not be great, but it's a helluva lot better than over there with the injured and dying," Deborah said.

"Sure is," Mary agreed. She was still feeling a bit guilty that she was going to sleep while Father Kapaun kept ministering.

Knowing they might be awakened at any time, they pushed the cots close together and lay down side by side. They smiled sleepily at each other.

"Goodnight, Mary."

"Goodnight, Deb."

They closed their eyes and within seconds managed to fall soundly asleep.

☆ ☆ ☆

The next morning, rays of sunshine crept in through the command post windows, but the mood of the battalion's officers was grim. The air support missions that had arrived overnight had broken up the Chinese assault, but the officers knew there were thousands of enemy soldiers preparing for another assault.

Outside, the remaining Americans were on the verge of losing control of the situation. The bursts of Chinese machine-guns and submachine guns were constant and the despair on the faces of the GIs showed that they all thought their situation was pretty much hopeless. There was no order, no more perimeter, no more commands. It was kill or be killed. The U.S. machine gunners could no longer fire in short bursts because of the sheer numbers of Chinese soldiers coming at them. Their machine-gun barrels began to heat up to a point that the rounds were swirling out of the barrels and falling short of their targets. There were not enough bullets left to kill the massive onslaught of the enemy coming toward the U.S. positions.

Chinese mortar rounds exploded around the command post. A mortar round made a large gaping hole in the back wall near where the grenade had exploded during the night. The sun poured in.

☆ ☆ ☆

Over in the jail cell, Mary and Deborah's eyes opened, immediately panicked by the sounds they heard. They jumped off their cots and huddled together.

"What was that?" Deborah asked.

"Sounded like another grenade," Mary replied.

"What do we do now?" Deborah yelled.

Mary thought for a second. "Hide!"

Mary slid under her cot as they continued to hear grenades and gunfire. Deborah quickly followed suit, both of them looking frightened to death. All they wanted was to be anywhere, anywhere but there.

☆ ☆ ☆

Father Kapaun tripped over a wounded man and fell out the command post's door. He stood wearily, and then he saw a GI shooting at a Chinese soldier. His gun jammed and the enemy soldier flung his bayonet into the GI's chest. Father Kapaun didn't react at first, simply gazing at the scene of hell on earth. Then he turned back to the post and searched out the Chinese officer. He yelled at him, "Make them stop! Enough already! No one in here is fighting back!"

131

The Chinese officer, Captain Yi, hesitated; then he nodded. He limped to the window and yelled in Mandarin, "Cease fire! Cease fire! This is Captain Yi of 115th CCF Division Chinese People's Army! There are only wounded in here!"

Within minutes, Chinese soldiers entered the command post. They pointed their weapons at everyone as the American soldiers and officers all reluctantly knew they had no chance to continue the battle. Surrender was not in their vocabulary.

The Chinese soldiers aided Captain Yi, moving him to a corner as they spoke with him quietly. During the discussions with them, he motioned to Father Kapaun and indicated that he was not to be harmed.

☆ ☆ ☆

The news quickly spread that the 3rd Battalion's command post had been overrun by Chinese forces.

Outside the command post, in a ditch some twenty yards away, a Chinese soldier found Sergeant Miller hiding under the dead soldier. He grabbed him and roughly pulled Miller out. The soldier put his rifle barrel right against the sergeant's forehead.

Sergeant Miller froze, awaiting his execution.

Kapaun was standing in the doorway of the command post and saw the whole thing. He broke away from his captors, ran up to the Chinese rifleman, and shoved the barrel away from Miller's head. He stared down at the Chinese soldier and said, "What is wrong with you?"

The surrounding Chinese soldiers looked stunned, but they held their fire. Father Kapaun held a hand out to Sergeant Miller and said, "Pappy, take my hand."

Sergeant Miller looked around, unsure what he should do. After a moment he reached up and took Father Kapaun's hand. Kapaun lifted Sergeant Miller up onto one foot, then lifted him onto his back, and carried him towards the command post. They joined a group of prisoners that had been assembled there.

The soldier who almost shot Sergeant Miller was completely dumbfounded. He stood and shook his rifle at Kapaun. The other Chinese soldiers didn't know what they were supposed to do. Some shrugged it off, but some of them got belligerent and started to shove the Americans around.

The first contingent of POWs was made to form up as a column and was marched away. As they struggled to keep up the pace the Chinese had set, they heard sporadic gunshots as many of the American soldiers, too wounded to walk, were methodically executed.

Interlude

Father Emil Kapaun Bio:

https://www.kapaun.org/about-us/history/father-kapaun   and
https://www.defense.gov/Explore/Features/story/Article/2539877/me
dal-of-honor-monday-army-chaplain-emil-j-kapaun/)

Emil Kapaun was born on April 20, 1916, on a farm in Pilsen, Kansas, about 60 miles north of Wichita to Elizabeth (Bessie) and Enos Kapaun. He enjoyed being outdoors, riding his bicycle, playing baseball, and spent many hours working on the family farm. He had one younger brother, Eugene, and attended the school and church at St. John Nepomucene in Pilsen.

He was ordained a priest on June 9, 1940 and served at his home parish of St. John Nepomucene in Pilsen, Kansas. After World War II broke out Kapaun was serving as an auxiliary chaplain at Herington Air Base, Kansas. In 1944, when he noticed the need for faith-based leaders in the military, he felt compelled to join up. So, on July 12, 1944, he became an Army chaplain, serving for the rest of World War II in the China-Burma-India theater.

When he returned to the U.S. in 1946, Kapaun separated from the Army to earn his master's degree in education from Catholic University in Washington, D.C., and then returned to the Diocese of Wichita to serve as a parish priest. Two years later, Father Kapaun sought permission to re-enter the Chaplain Corps. Bishop Mark K. Carroll agreed, and Father Kapaun was sent to Japan in 1949 as a captain.

A month after North Korea invaded South Korea in June of 1950, Father Kapaun and the 3rd Battalion, 8th Cavalry Regiment, 1st Cavalry Division were ordered to the Korean War to help repel the invasion. Father Kapaun became well-known for risking his life ministering to the soldiers on the front lines.

Calm Among Chaos
Excerpts of Father Kapaun Articles

By the fall of 1950, Kapaun's battalion had pushed the depleted North Korean soldiers back to Unsan, an area in northwestern North Korea near the Chinese border. It was assumed the war would soon be over since things were looking good for the U.S. and its South Korean allies. But on Nov. 1, 1950, the tide turned when Chinese Communist forces launched a vicious, massive surprise attack. About 20,000 soldiers pouring down on a few thousand Americans. In the chaos, dodging bullets and explosions, Father Kapaun raced between foxholes, out past the front lines and into no-man's land — dragging the wounded to safety.

When his commanders ordered an evacuation, Kapaun chose to stay, gathering the injured, tending to their wounds. When the enemy broke through and the combat was hand-to-hand, he carried on comforting the injured and the dying, offering some measure of peace as they left this earth.

With enemy forces baring down on the 3rd Battalion's command post, it seemed like the end was near and that any wounded Americans, more than a dozen of them, would be gunned down. But Father Kapaun spotted a wounded Chinese officer. He pleaded with this Chinese officer and convinced him to call out to his fellow Chinese. The shooting stopped and they negotiated a safe surrender, saving those American lives.

Prisoner of War Articles

Then, as Father Kapaun was being led away, he saw another American, Sgt. 1ˢᵗ Class Herbert A. Miller; wounded, unable to walk, laying in a ditch, defenseless. An enemy soldier was standing over him, rifle aimed at his head, ready to shoot. Father Kapaun marched over and pushed the enemy soldier aside. As the soldier watched, stunned, Father Kapaun carried the wounded American away.

An American who didn't fire a gun, but who wielded the mightiest weapon of all, a love for his brothers so pure that he was willing to die so that they might live. And yet, the incredible story of Father Kapaun does not end there. He carried that American for miles as their captors forced them on a death march. When Father Kapaun grew tired, he'd help the wounded soldier hop on one leg. When other prisoners stumbled, he picked them up. When they wanted to quit, knowing that stragglers would be shot, he begged them to keep walking.

In the camps that winter, deep in a valley, men could freeze to death in their sleep. Father Kapaun offered them his own clothes. They starved on tiny rations of millet, corn, and birdseed. He somehow snuck past the guards, foraged in nearby fields, and returned with rice and potatoes. In desperation, some men hoarded food. He convinced them to share. Their bodies were ravaged by dysentery. Kapaun grabbed some rocks, pounded metal scraps into pots and boiled clean water. They lived in filth. He washed their clothes, and he cleansed their wounds.

The guards ridiculed his devotion to his Savior and the Almighty. They took his clothes and made him stand in the freezing cold for hours on end. Yet, he never lost his faith. If anything, it only grew stronger. At night he slipped into huts to lead prisoners in prayer, saying the Rosary, administering the sacraments, offering three simple words: "God bless you." One of the prisoners later said that with his very presence he could just for a moment turn a mud hut into a cathedral.

That spring Father Kapaun held an Easter service. As the sun rose that Easter Sunday, he put on his purple stole and led dozens of prisoners to the ruins of an old church in the camp. And he read from a prayer missal that they had kept hidden. He held up a small crucifix that he had made from sticks. As the guards watched, Father Kapaun and all those prisoners, men of different faiths, perhaps some men of no faith, sang the Lord's Prayer and "America the Beautiful." They sang so loud that the other prisoners across the camp not only heard them, they joined in, too, filling the valley with song and prayer.

That faith, that they may be delivered from evil, that they could make it home, was perhaps the greatest gift to those men; that even amidst such hardship and despair, there could be hope; amid their misery in the temporal, they could see those truths that are eternal; that even in such hell, there could be a touch of the divine. Looking back, one of the prisoners said that that was is what "kept a lot of us alive."

Yet for Father Kapaun, the horrific conditions took their toll. Thin frail, he began to limp with a blood clot in his leg. And then came dysentery, then pneumonia. That's when the guards saw their chance to finally rid themselves of this priest and the hope he inspired. They came for him. Over the protests and tears of the men who loved him, the guards sent him to a death house—a hellhole with no food or water—to be left to die.

And yet, even then, his faith held firm. "I'm going to where I've always wanted to go," Father Kapaun told his brothers. "And when I get there, I'll say a prayer for all of you." Then, as he was being taken away, he did something remarkable, he blessed the guards. "Forgive them," he said, "for they know not what they do." Two days later, in that house of death, Father Kapaun breathed his last breath. His body was taken away, his grave unmarked, and his remains only recovered recently in the year 2021.

"I don't know the name of that valley, but we called it the Kapaun Valley because that is where Father Kapaun instilled in us a will to live," Korean War POW Mike Dowe said in 2013.

Never Losing Hope

While in captivity, Kapaun remained a trusted leader. His courage inspired prisoners of all faiths to survive the camp's hellish conditions and the frigid temperatures, resist enemy indoctrination, and keep hope alive. He helped the wounded and often sneaked out at night to steal food for the prisoners.

"He was the best food thief we had," Army Capt. Joseph O'Connor, a fellow POW, told The Corpus Christi Caller-Times after his repatriation in 1953. "He always used to say a prayer to St. Dismas [the penitent thief] before he went out scrounging. Once, he came back with a sack of potatoes. How he got it I'll never know — it must have weighed 100 pounds."

By spring, however, the camp's squalid conditions and inhumane punishments had taken their toll. Kapaun grew seriously ill and malnourished, but he managed to hold one last Easter Mass for the prisoners in late March. Shortly after that, he was transferred to an old pagoda that the Chinese called a hospital. It was unheated and filthy, and it was reported that its prisoners weren't given food or medical attention. Kapaun died there on May 23, 1951. He was 35.

April 12, 2013 — Secretary of the Army McHugh's remarks at Chaplain Kapaun <u>Hall of Heroes</u> Induction Ceremony

<u>https://www.army.mil/article/101285/april_12_2013_secarmy_mchughs_r emarks_at_chaplain_kapaun_hall_of_heroes_induction_ceremony</u>

To the Kapaun Family, Ray, and Lee, and so many others, cousins, nephews: Thank you. Not just for helping to bring this story to us, but for letting us share it in what I hope you are beginning to understand is such a special opportunity for us.

I had a chance to spend some time with the Chaplain's friends, his colleagues, his battle buddies, his spiritual buddies from the Korean Theater at lunch, incredible men, and we are so thrilled that they are here today helping us see the true story of a great American and a great American patriot.

Today, as the Chief [of Staff of the Army] said, truly are gathering to honor a remarkable soldier, a man of unquestioned and uncommon courage, and a man of truly unbridled faith, Army Chaplain, Captain Emil Kapaun.

Father Kapaun's name and exploits will be from this day forward, forever enshrined in the Hall of Heroes, a recipient of the Medal of Honor, our nation's highest military award.

And it probably goes without saying he joins a very elite company of American heroes, two of whom are with us here today who we deeply appreciate, who put self below service, who displayed acts of personal valor that truly were above and beyond the call of duty.

But as elite and as small that small band, that small company is among recipients of the Medal of Honor, Father Kapaun's story is, in itself, wholly unique, wholly different. He didn't charge a pillbox; he didn't defeat an enemy battalion or brigade or division by himself. Rather, Father Kapaun's only weapons were his steely defiance that inspired his fellow prisoners of war; the words he spoke, which brought comfort to the Soldiers with whom he served; and a simple piece of purple ribbon that he wore around his neck, a mark of his chaplaincy, his priesthood.

But don't make any mistake about it; Father Kapaun was a Soldier; and a Soldier in the purest, in the truest sense of the word.

He was a man who volunteered for service for Korea, even as he had already served his country in the Chaplain's Corp during World War II. During the Korean War, the good and brave father moved fearlessly under enemy fire to bring aid and comfort to the wounded and to the dying. And after being captured, he continued to lead, he continued to serve, securing food for starving POWs. And in so doing, feeding not just their bodies, but their souls and their spirits.

Reading Father Kapaun's story, I can't help but think he was part Audi Murphy and part Father Flanagan.

In his memoir, Murphy, who was also a Medal of Honor recipient, wrote that when a chaplain visited a company, and he prayed for what he described as "the strength of our arms and for the souls of the men...we do not consider his denomination. Helmets come off. Catholics, Jews, and Protestants bow their heads and finger their weapons." "It is," Murphy said, "front-line religion."

So it was, in that Korean prison camp, where Catholics, Protestants, Jews and Muslims, even those who declared no particular faith, drew courage, and drew strength and they drew hope from a priest, a priest who one survivor called the "best foot soldier" he had ever known.

To be sure, Father Kapaun was a man of contradictions. A man of faith, he was at the same time blunt. It is said he often cursed. A servant of God, he nevertheless stole food from his captors; and that was an act that troubled him — something he found at odds with his faith — even though because of it, unquestionably, many prisoners' lives were saved. Father Kapaun rectified this contradiction by praying to St. Dismas, the thief who, it is taught, was crucified at the right hand of Jesus Christ.

There's no question that he was a resourceful man, and that's a trait he may have perfected early in life. There's a story that's told that when the good Father was about seven years old, and not yet the good Father, it was determined that he was old enough to milk the family cow. Now, where I and Herb Miller come from in upstate New York, there are more cows than people, (Senator Roberts can talk about cows being from Kansas [laughter]. And getting to milk that family cow, I can tell you it was a pretty big deal. Of course, it was important to the family for another reason, it would free up Emil's mom to work more often in the fields with his dad. But that couldn't just happen. Before his mom could really hand over the reins, or hand over the udders in this case, she needed to train Emil on the proper way to milk the cow. And the training from mom to son, by all accounts, went very, very well. And finally, his mom felt confident enough to hand over responsibility for milking that cow to that 7-year-old young man.

On his first day without his mother's supervision, Emil led the cow to a fence post, tied the cow up, just as his mom had taught him. But that cow refused to be milked. Every time, and at every angle, that little Emil tried to approach the cow, the cow would just step away. Emil stood there for a moment, he stared at the cow — as seven-year-olds are prone to do — trying to figure out how to make it all work, and then it hit him. The problem was that the cow wasn't used to seeing him, it was used to seeing his mom. So, he went into the house, put on one of his mom's dresses, came out, milked the cow. Problem solved [laughter]. Resourcefulness even at such a young age.

Much later, as we all know now, Father Kapaun was entered into the process for Sainthood in the Catholic Church, where he has been declared a Servant of God.

Under Fire: Army Chaplains in Korea, 1950

https://www.army.mil/article/100572/under_fire_army_chaplains_in
_korea_1950

WASHINGTON (April 9, 2013) — The start of hostilities in Korea during June 1950 caught most American officials off guard, and those in charge of the U.S. Army Chaplain Corps were no exception.

For the previous five years, America's military focus had been on divesting itself of the huge force that had been employed during World War Two. There were 8,141 Army chaplains on active duty as that war ended in 1945; by the end of 1947, only a little more than 1,100 remained. Nearly 500 of those transferred to the recently established U.S. Air Force in 1949. On the eve of the North Korean attack on South Korea, there were 706 active-duty Army chaplains, with more in the National Guard and U.S. Army Reserve.

With war again a reality in 1950, the Army had to rapidly expand. Having just gone through the painful process of involuntarily releasing chaplains from active duty and forcing them into reserve status, the Chaplain Corps now had to reverse the process and recall reserve chaplains to active duty. Chaplain authorizations would more than double in the coming years, topping out at 1,618 in 1953.

Even though numerous chaplains entered the active force through reserve component mobilizations, individual recalls, and an intense recruiting effort, the number of chaplains serving never matched what was authorized. Many veterans of World War Two were understandably reluctant to volunteer for combat duty again, and popular support for the war would wane during its final years as the conflict devolved into a stalemate.

While America mobilized in 1950, America's Army went to war. The first American ground forces to deploy to Korea were the divisions that had been stationed in Japan as occupation forces following World War Two. In trying to stem the tide that was the North Korean invasion of South Korea, many hastily deployed American units found themselves in desperate situations; it often came down to more of a battle for survival than it was an attempt to inflict harm on the enemy. Chaplains assigned to those units found themselves spending far more time comforting the wounded and praying for the fallen—and trying to evade capture—than they did in ministering to the living.

The first chaplain to serve in Korea deployed there with the initial American ground force to enter the conflict: Task Force Smith, an under-strength battalion of the 24th Infantry Division's 21st Infantry Regiment. The battalion's chaplain, Carl R. Hudson, had been looking forward to a routine tour of garrison duty in Japan upon his assignment to the unit a few weeks beforehand. Chaplain Hudson and the rest of the task force's 540 soldiers had little time to do anything after settling into a defensive position just north of the town of Osan during the early morning hours of July 5, 1950.

A large force of North Korean tanks and infantry attacked just a few hours later. By early afternoon, the task force was completely overrun, its survivors scattered. Chaplain Hudson, along with the battalion's surgeon and a large group of walking wounded, spent most of the following night and day making their way southward to the safety of the nearest American unit.

Other chaplains of the 24th Infantry Division had experiences similar to that of Hudson during that difficult month of July 1950, narrowly escaping as one American position after another fell before the North Korean advance. All survived, with the exception of Chaplain Herman G. Felhoelter of the 19th Infantry Regiment.

With his battalion falling back as the American position along the Kum River collapsed, Felhoelter volunteered to remain behind with a group of critically wounded men. A North Korean patrol came upon the group and executed the prostrate soldiers and their praying chaplain. Felhoelter was the first of twelve chaplains to die in action or as a prisoner during the Korean War. The second also perished in July 1950, when Chaplain Byron D. Lee of the 35th Infantry Regiment (25th Infantry Division) was mortally wounded during an attack from an enemy aircraft.

Amazingly enough, no chaplains were captured during those confusing initial months of the Korean War despite all the American setbacks. That would change within a few months, however. After the front stabilized at the Pusan Perimeter and then the Inchon Invasion changed the strategic focus of the war, during the final months of 1950 American units and other forces of the United Nations Command no longer retreated but instead advanced deep into North Korean territory. China entered the war in October 1950, when American and South Korean troops approached the Yalu River, the border between Korea and China.

The first major American-Chinese clash took place near the town of Unsan during the first week of November when a powerful Chinese attack overwhelmed the 1st Cavalry Division's 8th Cavalry Regiment. The regiment's battered 1st and 2nd battalions managed to withdraw, but the 3rd battalion was surrounded and largely annihilated. The 3rd battalion's chaplain, Emil J. Kapaun, was captured.

The 1950 Chinese counteroffensive generated heavy casualties on both sides. Within a month of Kapaun's capture, three more chaplains also became prisoners of war: Kenneth C. Hyslop (19th Infantry Regiment), Wayne H. Burdue (2nd Engineer Battalion, 2nd Infantry Division), and Lawrence F. Brunnert (32nd Infantry Regiment, 7th Infantry Division). Two other chaplains were killed during those weeks: Samuel R. Simpson (38th Infantry Regiment, 2nd Infantry Division) and James W. Conner (31st Infantry Regiment, 7th Infantry Division). The fate of the four captured chaplains was unknown until the release of surviving American prisoners in 1953. Sadly, none of the four chaplain POWs survived their incarcerations.

For the opening battles of the Korean War, as with most wars, those who are already in uniform at the start of the conflict bore the burden of the opening battles. The eight chaplains lost in 1950 were all members of the pre-war Chaplain Corps. Six were veterans of World War Two. Burdue, Lee, and Simpson had served continuously since the 1940s without a break in service. Hyslop, Kapaun, and Felhoelter also served in World War Two but were released from active duty in 1946. Within two years, however, they decided to continue their service to God and country; all three volunteered for recall to active duty in 1948. Conner and Brunnert joined the others in the pre-war era, being commissioned in 1948 and 1949, respectively.

None of these eight veteran chaplains knew what the year 1950 would bring, but all rose to the challenges that came with ministering to Soldiers under fire. Only a few received public recognition for the actions that ultimately cost them their lives: Conner was awarded the Silver Star, Felhoelter the Distinguished Service Cross, and Kapaun received numerous awards.

Kapaun will be posthumously awarded the Medal of Honor by President Barack Obama, April 11, 2013, at the White House.

All eight earned the undying thanks and gratitude of the Soldiers they served — the only award for which any of them would have asked.

Revered by All

In August 1951, Kapaun was honored with the Distinguished Service Cross, the nation's second highest medal for valor, while he was still listed as missing in action. Officials learned of his death when his fellow POWs were released after the armistice was signed in 1953. For decades, Kapaun's comrades lobbied Congress to get his Distinguished Service Cross upgraded to the Medal of Honor. On April 11, 2013, that request was granted. President Barack Obama lauded the chaplain's service during a While House ceremony.

"[Kapaun was] an American soldier who didn't fire a gun but who wielded the mightiest weapon of all — the love for his brothers — so pure that he was willing to die so they might live," President Obama said.

Now back to the story...

Part Two — Prisoner of War

"War is peace.
Freedom is slavery.
Ignorance is strength."
— George Orwell, 1984

"War is what happens when language fails."

— Margaret Atwood

Chapter 10

November 2, 1950

Unsan

Mary and Deborah slid out from under the cots in the jail cell, crept over to the window, and peeked out, trying to see what was happening outside without being seen. From their vantage point, they saw several wounded American soldiers being shot and others marched away, guns pointed at them. A Chinese soldier looked back in their direction, and they quickly ducked down, looking at each other, panic-stricken.

"You think he saw us?" Deborah asked.

"I sure as hell hope not," Mary said.

"What do we do now?" Deborah asked, nearly in tears.

Mary wanted to look out the window again to see if anyone was coming, but she knew it wasn't worth the risk. She looked at Deborah who was waiting for her to answer. Mary sighed and said, "Nothing to do now but stay hidden and hope they don't come back for us."

Deborah nodded, her face a mask of fear. "Okay," she sobbed.

Father Kapaun carried Sergeant Pappy Miller as the Chinese soldiers forced them to march down the rutted road headed north into captivity. Sergeant Bill Richardson, Lieutenant Mike Dowe, PFC Tibor Rubin, Doc Anderson, Captain William Shadish, PFC Patrick Schuler, Lieutenant Bill Funchess, Sergeant Vincent Doyle, PFC Peter Busatti, Lieutenant Ralph Nardella, Lieutenant Bob Wood, and PFC Joe Ramirez followed behind Father Kapaun with more than a dozen other soldiers limping along behind them.

PFC Joe Ramirez, having been hit several times, was not in a good way and nearly passed out. He started to fall behind the POW column. A Chinese soldier barked something at Ramirez he didn't understand, but he understood the sentiment. He quickened his pace, afraid of getting shot again.

As he caught up with the rear of the column, a soldier fell down in front of Ramirez. He leaned over, picked the man up, and looped the soldier's arm over his shoulder just to keep him walking. After a few minutes, the man removed his arm and limped along on his own. Then Joe hurried his pace and caught up with Father Kapaun.

Pappy said, "Father, you should put me down. I think I can walk. I don't want to be a burden to you."

"Son, if I put you down, they'll put you down. And I won't have that. Understand?"

Pappy nodded, nearly in tears, touched by what the man was doing for him.

"You realize you're saving my life? That if it wasn't for you, I'd either have frozen to death or been shot. Maybe both," Pappy said.

Father Kapaun said, "No one is going to shoot you. I won't allow it. And as long as we keep walking, we'll stay warm."

Pappy nodded and turned his eyes to the sky, mouthing "Thank you" to God.

Joe caught up with Father Kapaun and said, "Have you seen —"

Joe's question was interrupted by the sound of a single shot. He continued to walk as he turned around and saw the man he'd previously helped up and who had looked all right, lying on the side of the road behind him, a bullet in his back. The Chinese soldier, turned executioner, kicked the corpse and walked on as if shooting the man were nothing.

Father Kapaun, who did not turn around but continued walking, asked Joe, "Seen who?"

Joe was freaked out and said, "Talk about it later. They're shooting people who can't keep up."

"So, let's do everything we can to keep up. We have no other choice," Father Kapaun said.

"Yes, Father."

They continued walking. Joe fell a little behind Father Kapaun as his brain started working overtime, trying to think of a way out of the hopeless situation, but no ideas came.

Suddenly two American fighter planes roared overhead, flying too fast and too high in the sky for the pilots to notice anyone below. But the Chinese soldiers looked worried all the same.

Off to the right was a small farmhouse. The Chinese soldiers began pushing everyone towards the farmhouse as quickly as they could, shooting the ones who didn't move fast enough until they were all standing just outside the door to the farmhouse.

Inside the farmhouse, a Chinese soldier screamed something in Chinese to a Korean mother who stood with her husband and daughter as the soldier pointed at a door.

The woman looked furious and yelled at the soldier in Korean, "No boots in house. No boots."

The Chinese soldier waved them away until the three of them disappeared into a bedroom and closed the door behind them.

☆ ☆ ☆

That night, in the main room of the farmhouse, Chinese soldiers armed with submachine guns paced back and forth on one side of the room, keeping an eye on the bootless POWs on the other.

Lieutenant Wood moved close to Sergeant Richardson and said, "Bill, if I can get through that door, I can find a way out of here." Wood looked like he was ready to leap up and run.

In basic training, all new recruits are taught that if they are captured, it is an Order and Directive to escape from and evade the enemy. It is their duty to escape and take as many of their soldiers with them. Drill Sergeants didn't tell recruits 'how' to escape other than to 'improvise, plan, seek the right moment and run for your lives.' In other words, get out as best you can. No further details were given in training.

Bill rolled his eyes and said, "And just how far do you think you'll get before they blow your head off, Bob?"

Lieutenant Wood shrugged and said, "We need to do something. We're like fish in a barrel here."

"We can't afford to lose anyone else, especially not a soldier of your caliber. Does that make sense?" Bill asked.

"It does. Thanks, Bill. You're right as usual," Bob said.

Bob walked a few steps away. The Chinese soldiers raised their guns. He quickly sat down and looked up at the ceiling.

Lieutenant Dowe, sitting next to Bill, leaned over and whispered, "Did you have a plan of your own?"

"Not yet. But if you have something a little more thought out than what Bob had, let me know and we'll run it by Captain Shadish," Bill said.

"Will do," Mike said, leaning back against the wall, lost in thought. It wasn't about a plan, however. He was thinking about his father and reflecting on the fact that the last letter he'd written home hadn't been cheerier.

PFC Joe Ramirez and Father Kapaun sat nearby. Joe looked around nervously, tried to get Father Kapaun's attention, wanting to make sure the Chinese weren't listening though he didn't know how much they could understand.

"Hey, Father, I was wondering if you knew what happened to Mary and Deb?" Joe asked.

Father Kapaun thought about it for a moment, smiled, and replied, "Actually, I sent them to jail."

Joe looked confused. "Jail?"

Father Kapaun laughed softly and said, "Relax. They should be fine there."

Joe nodded and smiled, suddenly understanding what Father Kapaun meant.

"You probably saved their lives," Joe said.

"I hope so," Father Kapaun replied.

The nurses had made their way to the command post, stepping around the dead Chinese and Americans. No one was still alive. There was nothing they could do about the dead. They went into the command post and found the radio. Mary sat near the radio manipulating the buttons. The radio played static loudly, but nothing else. The women looked weary and frustrated.

"Why can't you reach anyone?" Deborah asked.

Mary sighed and replied, "I think the Chinese must have broken the radio before they left."

"Why would they do that?" Deborah asked.

Mary gave her a look and Deborah suddenly got it. She felt like a fool for even asking such a question.

"I guess that makes sense," Deborah replied sheepishly.

Mary continued to fiddle with the dials on the radio.

Deborah looked around, checking out everything around them. After a moment she perked up and said, "At least there's food!"

She jumped up, grabbed a hunk of bread, and stuffed it in her mouth, chewing on it like she hadn't eaten in a month. After swallowing the first few bites, she stopped chewing long enough to look at Mary. "You want some?"

Mary frowned and replied, "I'm good. Not sure I'm up to eating anything right now with everything going on."

Deborah shook her head and said, "All right." She started chewing on the bread again.

"I just hope everyone's okay," Mary said.

Deborah stopped chewing, suddenly feeling the guilt of being alive that she realized Mary must be feeling as well. She looked at Nurse Mary and nodded, swallowing the rest of the food in her mouth with a now dry throat, and taking a seat across from Mary. She no longer felt hungry.

☆ ☆ ☆

The POWs still sat around the living room of the farmhouse, still bootless and bored out of their minds. The boredom was balanced by the fear of what was going to happen. They heard a fighter plane roar by outside. Some looked hopeful, but most either ignored it or didn't even have the mental capacity to hear it right then.

Tibor Rubin looked at Doc Anderson and asked quietly, "Are they going to make us sit here all day? What's going on?"

"Actually, they are," Doc replied. He shifted a little. He didn't want the Chinese soldiers to become too attentive.

Sergeant Vincent Doyle and Rubin exchanged confused looks. Vincent turned to Doc and meekly asked, "Why?"

"I overheard them talking about not wanting us to be seen by the fighter planes," Doc responded.

"You speak Chinese?" PFC Schuler asked.

"A little."

"How do you tell them to go to hell in Chinese?" PFC Peter Busatti asked.

"You don't," Doc replied, frowning at Busatti like he was an idiot.

Lieutenant Ralph Nardella saw a couple of Chinese soldiers approaching them from across the room and whispered, "Quiet, here they come."

Everyone leaned back, acting as nonchalant as they could. They had no idea how much English the soldiers could understand, but they weren't about to give away anything.

A Chinese soldier looked them over like he was trying to see what they were up to. No one made eye contact with him. After a while, he turned and walked away.

Lieutenant Mike Dowe's eyes grew wide. Rubin noticed the lieutenant's reaction and looked all around. Rubin turned to the lieutenant and asked, "What is it?"

"Asshole's wearing my boots," Lieutenant Dowe said, looking disgusted.

Everyone looked around, realizing the Chinese soldiers were wearing the Americans' boots.

☆ ☆ ☆

That night, the POWs were forced to march down the road by the light of the moon. Most were bootless and struggled to stay on the road even with numerous Chinese soldiers surrounding them and pushing and shoving them back into formation.

As Father Kapaun marched, he prayed loud enough for those around him to hear but quiet enough that the Chinese soldiers could not. "Yea, though I walk through the valley of the shadow of death, I shall fear no evil: For thou art with me ..."

☆ ☆ ☆

Mary and Deborah sat by the radio inside the abandoned 3rd battalion command post as the one remaining radio continued to buzz at them.

Deborah said crossly, "Will you turn that stupid thing off?"

Mary sighed and said, "I guess I might as well. At some point, we may need to start walking out of here. I just hope we don't get captured. I'm not built for that shit."

Mary turned the radio off and sat back down. She looked at Deborah and shook her head.

"You really think we could get captured?" Deborah asked.

Mary shrugged, exasperated. "What do you think? We're all alone in a savage country. All the men, wounded or not, have been taken. Probably half of them were shot."

Deborah asked with a deep frown, "What do you think they'd do to us if they captured us? I mean, we're not soldiers. You think they'd let us go?"

Mary shook her head and said, "Why would they capture us if they were just going to let us go? I don't want to even think about what they might do to us. Can we change the subject?"

Deborah nodded, anxious to talk about something else, anything else.

Suddenly they heard a whooping sound coming from outside; both women looked frightened.

"Is that them? Are they coming to get us now?" Deborah asked.

Mary, staying low, ran to the window and looked out. Outside, a U.S. helicopter was setting down in the middle of the camp.

Mary, smiling from ear to ear, turned to Deborah. "We're saved!"

"What?" Deborah asked, running to the window and looking out. She saw the helicopter and both women began jumping up and down, hugging each other.

Mary opened the window and shouted, "We're in here!"

The pilot and the soldiers with him looked at Mary. They looked confused. They hadn't seen any living person when they set down.

The nurses ran outside.

"Thank God you came! I didn't think we were going to make it," Mary said, gleeful.

"How many people are with you?" the pilot asked.

"It's just the two of us," Deborah replied.

The pilot and soldiers looked back and forth at one another, trying to take it all in.

Finally, the pilot shook his head, offered the biggest smile he could manage, and said, "Okay, jump in. Let's get you out of here!"

Mary and Deborah ran to the helicopter and climbed in.

☆ ☆ ☆

The POWs continued to march for several days. Always at night. They slept in random dilapidated buildings during the day until it was time to get up and begin marching again. They were given small amounts of water and old bread. The men were beginning to lose strength. Some were dying of their festering wounds.

A truck picked them up from a building that had been nearly burnt to the ground, and the POWs were thrilled that they no longer had to walk. But within minutes of the truck taking off with a load of Americans, it broke down, and they were once again made to march by the light of the moon, bootless, starving, and losing their strength quickly.

Some of the POWs no longer had the energy to go on. Each time one soldier fell behind, he was killed. The Americans were shot in the back and left to die on the side of the road. Father Kapaun said a silent prayer for each. The rest of the POWs marched on without them, struggling to gather enough energy to keep themselves alive. The fear staggered them as they made their way to who knew where.

☆ ☆ ☆

As the sun began to rise on November 28, 1950, the POWs entered the village of Sombokal, North Korea. The locals were not happy with the new arrivals and showed their displeasure at seeing them. Both men and women spat at the POWs. Some threw rocks at them.

A North Korean officer, Lee Tse-Sung, a man in his thirties, greeted the POWs just inside the village. "We welcome to this temporary camp despite the reactions of the local peoples. We will correct the errors in your thinking, and you will see them as peace-loving peoples that they are. Don't think of yourselves as captives, but as liberated."

The POWs looked around at the villagers, who were still spitting and throwing rocks at them. The captives wiped the spit off themselves and did their best not to get hit in the face with a rock. Peace-loving people indeed.

Chapter 11

November 28, 1950
Sombokal

Father Kapaun and thirty POWs sat in a disgusting pigsty in the temporary prisoner of war camp in Sombokal. They were exhausted, hungry, scared, and out of options.

Lieutenant Ralph Nardella asked Father Kapaun, "What do you think they're gonna do to us next, Father?"

"Probably shoot the officers and let the enlisted men go," Father Kapaun replied.

Lieutenant Nardella's eyes grew wide and his mouth fell open. Father Kapaun laughed and said, "Come on, Ralph. They can take away our freedom, but they can't take away our sense of humor, too."

Everyone nearby laughed weakly. Lieutenant Nardella eventually laughed, too.

"Boy, you had me going there for a minute, Father," Lieutenant Nardella said, still chuckling.

Father Kapaun smiled. He pulled out his pipe, taped together many times over, and a pouch of Prince Albert tobacco. He remembered each time he'd had to tape it. Those moments now seemed precious. Moments where he was blessed by good fortune.

"You guys want a little puff of this? If so, you might as well have it now because what I've got isn't going to last much longer," Father Kapaun offered.

"I'll take a puff," Sergeant Vincent Doyle said.

Father Kapaun nodded at Vincent and handed him the pipe. Doyle took several puffs from the pipe before handing it back, looking happy.

☆ ☆ ☆

A layer of snow covered the ground of the POW camp as flurries moved through the air. Father Kapaun walked around outside with no jacket, boots, or winter gear. Tragically, many of the POWs in the camp were suffering: their feet were turning black from frostbite.

About 400 frozen dead bodies were stacked up like cordwood just yards away from their meager quarters. Father Kapaun looked at the frozen dead bodies and shook his head, walking on. He'd blessed them already. They were in God's hands now. Nothing more he could do.

After taking several steps away from the stack of dead bodies, Father Kapaun scrounged through a trash pile near some abandoned pig stalls and found a piece of tin. He carefully turned the edges up by putting it in between the slats of the pig stall and created a rudimentary bowl. Looking carefully around for any guards, he felt in his pockets and came up with a match. He made an illegal fire and began heating up snow to make water.

Lieutenant Bill Funchess, wearing only one boot, walked by, stopping when he saw what Father Kapaun was doing, looking at the water as if he couldn't believe what he was seeing.

Father Kapaun saw him walk over, looked at the one boot, and started to say something, but changed his mind. Lieutenant

Funchess stared at the water, looking like he was out of his mind thirsty. He couldn't even remember what clean, clear water tasted like. Kapaun quietly asked, "Would you like a drink of water?"

"I'd love one!" Lieutenant Funchess replied. Father Kapaun shushed him.

Lieutenant Funchess grabbed the bowl, took a large gulp, and nearly swooned as if he was in Heaven.

"Good?" Father Kapaun asked.

"That was amazing. I don't remember the last time I had even a sip of water," Lieutenant Funchess replied.

Father Kapaun extended his hand and said, "I'm Father Kapaun."

They shook hands.

"Lieutenant Bill Funchess. I know who you are. I've seen you around. You seem to be everyone's hero. Mine too, now," Lieutenant Funchess said.

They smiled at one another.

"Where're you from?" Father Kapaun asked.

"South Carolina. And you?"

"I'm from Kansas. I'm headed to the enlisted area now to offer prayers and help to the GIs. Regardless of what the guards say."

"Well, if the guards ever take away your Bible, Father, I have a pocket one hidden in the bandages of my foot."

"Really?" Father Kapaun asked, looking surprised.

"Yeah. Don't think they'll ever find it there," Lieutenant Funchess said, laughing.

Father Kapaun looked at Bill's untreated, wounded foot and said, "Thanks. Don't let these Chinese wear you down. Keep your spirits up. Once your foot heals, you'll be running circles around them."

"I like the sound of that," Lieutenant Funchess said.

Father Kapaun walked off. Before he got very far, he ran into Dick Halgen They stood together and watched as a POW Father Kapaun was not familiar with was forced to strip in the freezing air; then he was soundly beaten with a stick as the guards poured cold water over him. The icicles immediately formed all over his body. He turned blue. Kapaun knew there could be no reason why he was beaten. The enemy just felt like it.

Father Kapaun shook his head and said under his breath, "So glad the girls didn't end up here."

"What's that, Father?" Dick asked.

Father Kapaun looked at him and shook his head. "Nothing."

Father Kapaun walked off, still shaking his head and thinking about Mary and Deborah, hoping that wherever they'd ended up they were all right.

☆ ☆ ☆

Nurses Mary and Deborah sat in a small, bare room in Quantico, Virginia, with Sergeant McClusky of Army Intelligence who had been speaking to the nurses and taking a lot of notes. He reread his notes as Mary and Deborah glanced somewhat nervously at each other. Deborah took a sip from the now lukewarm cup of white coffee in front of her.

Sergeant McClusky cleared his throat, looked back at the nurses, and asked, "So you don't know the actual date the Chinese captured the troops in your command post?"

Deborah shrugged.

Mary furrowed her brow and replied, "Not exactly. It was sometime in early November."

"November?" McClusky asked.

"Yes, I remember because it wasn't long after Father Kapaun said mass on All Saint's Day," Mary replied.

McClusky wrote this down, looked at Mary, and said, "Interesting. And why did you not radio anyone and let them know what had happened?"

"I told you already," Mary said. "The radio was broken. All we got was static."

McClusky nodded and said, "That's right. Sorry, I forgot."

He closed his notebook, smiled at the nurses, and said, "Thank you for your time. I only wish we would have gotten there sooner and stopped this from happening. Have a good day, ladies. I'm so happy you made it through this terrible ordeal."

He got up and left the room.

Mary and Deborah looked at each other feeling both shocked and relieved.

"What an asshole," Deborah said.

Mary said, "It wasn't that bad. Besides, at least we're back home again. I hope they give us some leave now."

Deborah nodded and said, "Thank God for that!"

☆ ☆ ☆

The night was particularly cold even for North Korea in winter. The sky was clear, the stars sharp against the blanket of black. Father Kapaun shivered as he sat on a cot in a crowded hut, smoking his pipe. He watched his breath in the cold air. Rows and rows of men were packed tightly together, sleeping spoon fashion, with their cold feet clamped in the armpits of others.

The next morning Father Kapaun slept on his cot while, behind him, Lieutenant Funchess opened his eyes and sat bolt upright. He looked around, his eyes wide, on the verge of screaming.

"My God!" Lieutenant Funchess yelled, horrified. He realized that the men on either side of him were dead, frozen during the night.

Father Kapaun sat up and looked over at the source of the scream. He saw Lieutenant Funchess with the two dead bodies surrounding him. As he started to get up to help Funchess, Father Kapaun heard something behind him and spun around. It was Dick Halgen, lying on his cot, coughing up blood.

Father Kapaun went to Dicks's side and tried to help him, but he could already tell that it was too late. Father Kapaun delivered the last rites, holding Dick up to keep him from choking more on his blood. Moments later, Dick died in Father Kapaun's arms. He wasn't the first man to die so and Father Kapaun knew he wouldn't be the last.

An hour later, Father Kapaun stood at the burial ground using the only tools he had, dog tags and sticks, to dig a hole to bury Dick Halgen.

Dicks's dead body lay next to the hole Father Kapaun was attempting to dig. He'd dragged the body from the hut with the help of Funchess. So far, the hole was all of two inches deep in the snow-covered ground and Father Kapaun struggled to make a bigger dent in the frozen ground. He had a long way to go.

Chinese guards watched Father Kapaun dig, their faces impassive, lacking compassion. Behind Father Kapaun was a stack now containing nearly 1,500 bodies. There were so many more bodies than the stack he'd seen just a day earlier; it was overwhelming.

Father Kapaun continued to dig, not wanting to toss Dick's body up there with the hundreds of other nameless, faceless bodies. If he could bury just one, just one, he prayed, he would have brought some dignity to the world.

As the prisoners mustered their strength, some joined Kapaun and after several hours of effort were able to dig a shallow grave. Father Kapaun proceeded to perform a brief burial mass for this lost soldier, another testament to the callous nature of communism.

☆ ☆ ☆

On the morning of Christmas Day, Bessie Kapaun stood in front of the Christmas tree in their front parlor. The Christmas tree was beautiful. It was large, filled with many lights and decorations with a few nicely wrapped presents underneath. But Bessie's face was only a mask of sadness and worry.

Enos brought her an egg nog and she took it, holding it in her hands as she continued to stare blankly at the Christmas tree.

"What do you think Emil is doing now?" she asked.

"I'm sure he's getting ready to spend Christmas with the men he's had at his side these last several months. Not to mention, he's probably really missing his mother something terrible," Enos said.

Bessie sighed, sipped her egg nog, and continued looking at the tree.

"I just hope he's all right," she said. "We haven't heard from him in quite a while. That's just not like him."

Enos slipped his arm around Bessie and said, "I'm sure he's fine. I wouldn't be surprised if he was back here in a few weeks."

Bessie managed a weak smile and said, "That would be lovely."

Enos smiled at Bessie and gently kissed her on the cheek.

It was nighttime on December 25, 1950. The POWs were taken to a large, drafty barn. Even though this was a novelty, every man looked like he couldn't care less about whatever it was that was about to happen. Not only was this the worst Christmas any of the men had ever experienced; each man was only too aware of his own mortality.

The POWs were seated on the rough wooden floor of the barn. In front of them was a warped raised stage. On the stage, the Communists had assembled an ensemble of young local boys and girls to perform for the captives.

The children performed a hammer and sickle song while doing what Kapaun recognized as a "harvesting of the crops" dance. Everything had an obvious Communist message to it. The POWs were not moved by the entertainment. But despite their indifference, they had no choice but to sit there and not let the guards see how bored they were for fear that they could be removed from the barn, taken outside, and executed.

At what appeared to be the intermission, some of the prisoners put their heads together and began singing "Silent Night, Holy Night." As their prayerful chorus carried throughout the barn, the volume increased. One after another, more voices joined in "... all is calm, all is bright ..."

The POWs looked around, amazed that they were getting away with this. The Korean children knew it was Christmas! They sang along and the combined voices converged in the closing words "... sleep in heavenly peace."

The guards were furious. They blew their whistles furiously and hustled the children off the stage. The evening's performance was over, and the guards were angry, but every one of the POWs was smiling.

Shortly after Christmas, the POWs were marched out of Sombokal. They passed stacks of frozen prisoners' bodies, five high, with arms and legs sticking out unceremoniously. Many soldiers could not even look at the horrific sight.

As the POWs were marched, now in broad daylight and in the freezing cold with no winter gear, several stragglers fell out and were quickly murdered by the North Korean guards.

Father Kapaun wore his helmet liner while helping fellow POWs on the march. The guards taunted him, throwing rocks at his head, and laughing, but Father Kapaun paid them no mind. He marched on, pretending they were not even there.

The few remaining POWs looked like hell, as they were marched into a bombed-out mountain town that bordered the Yalu River. It was still freezing cold, and the bodies were already stacked up in Prisoner of War Camp #5 in Pyoktong, North Korea. About 800 Western POWs were already imprisoned there.

The camp was mainly mud huts and a few larger buildings that were used for camp services. A former Buddhist temple was now a "hospital" and there was a bombed-out Protestant Church.

At the far end of the camp, a stretch of the frozen Yalu river was accessible. China was on the other side. Given the town's position on the border with China, it was obvious to Father Kapaun that the bombing was down to the US Air Force's attempts to interdict the movement of men and supplies coming across the river.

The following morning camp guard Kim Wong stood over Father Kapaun, gun pointed at him, forcing him to sit on the frozen river wearing only his underwear. Father Kapaun shivered violently.

"Where is your God now? Let him come and take you from here!" Wong asked as he prodded Kapaun with the butt of his rifle.

Doc Anderson, wearing only his underwear as well, and carrying what remained of his uniform approached with the Chinese political officer, Comrade Sun, following him.

Comrade Sun looked at Father Kapaun and said, "Now do you see why you must live in the officer's camp? If you refuse, you will live here, on this frozen river with only your helmet liner to draw heat from."

"As a chaplain, it is my duty to tend to the needs of all POWs, enlisted and officers alike," Father Kapaun firmly stated, his teeth nonetheless chattering. "This is in the Geneva Conventions."

"Officers are forbidden from going near the enlisted camp. Get dressed!" Comrade Sun ordered.

Father Kapaun and Doc Anderson dressed quickly in their rags and began to walk barefoot back to the camp.

"As a doctor, I must be allowed to treat patients at the hospital. It's my duty," Doc told Comrade Sun.

"And I must also be able to give these men the support they so badly need in these horrible times," Father Kapaun added.

"What these men need is medicine and study. Not prayer," Comrade Sun said smugly.

"They're not getting a lot of medicine so a little prayer wouldn't hurt," Father Kapaun said, challenging Comrade Sun as much as he could.

"Kapaun, do not make me repeat myself. Only Doc can go to hospital. And you are not permitted to spread your poisonous Christian propaganda here," Comrade Sun said adamantly.

"I see a lot of men go into the hospital, but not many come out?" Doc asked, careful to turn his accusation into a question.

"Everyone who's died there has died of natural causes," Comrade Sun assured him.

"At nineteen?" Doc questioned, glaring at Comrade Sun.

"If they are sick, it is because of a disease previously contracted. Our doctors know what they are doing. I'm told you treated a Chinese officer in battle at Unsan," Comrade Sun said.

"As a doctor, I've taken an oath to help anyone who is sick," Doc said, defending himself.

"That is what is wrong with your people. They teach you *how* to cure, not *who* to cure," Comrade Sun stated.

"Our men are walking around sick and wounded, dying by the dozens, and you think by starving us you'll convert us to Communism?" Father Kapaun asked.

Comrade Sun held up his thumb and finger a quarter of an inch apart and said, "If we can sow this much doubt in your minds, we win."

Disgusted, Father Kapaun threw his helmet liner in the trash heap and kept walking.

They began to pass the Chinese-run hospital, a tile-roofed former Buddhist monastery partially bombed-out, the outside painted ornately with birds and animals. Father Kapaun and Doc looked at the building, glanced at each other, shook their heads.

Suddenly they heard a dull roar and they all looked up. A flight of four American F-80C Shooting Stars flew overhead, slower than usual.

Comrade Sun yelled, "Everyone, get out of the open. Now!"

Comrade Sun, Wong, and several guards ran off, scattering for cover. Father Kapaun and Doc Anderson used the distraction to run inside the nearby hospital.

Father Kapaun and Doc Anderson entered the hospital holding their noses. The stench was nauseating; the scene that met their eyes horrific.

Patients had been laid on mud floors in their own excrement; there were no beds or bedding in the entire place. It appeared that the patients had been abandoned to die from the infections in their wounds. One entire room was filled with patients who appeared afflicted with dysentery.

"This isn't a hospital. It's a death house," Doc said. He ached to work on the men, but knew he couldn't do a thing. They had very little medicine, no instruments, no nurses, not even basic hygiene. He wasn't even sure where he would begin.

Father Kapaun walked over to a dying patient and administered the last rites. He finished and joined Doc, standing still in shock, looking at the sick and dying patients.

"No wonder Sun didn't want you to see this place. He didn't want you to see the truth," Doc said.

Father Kapaun shook his head and said, "Lies are the only truth they know." Again, recognizing the inhumanity of the communist creed.

"Ain't that the truth," Doc confirmed as they continued to look around at the diseased prisoners.

Chapter 12

January 1, 1951
Pyoktong, North Korea

The winter days dragged on, endlessly. The intense cold continued to claim lives. Each day, young men of many nations were sacrificed for an ideology. Early one morning a convoy of vehicles bearing red stars entered the camp with the camp guards hurrying to line its route.

An hour later a large crowd of POWs sat in the assembly area of the barn, bored out of their minds, and surrounded by numerous guards.

General Fang finished giving a speech in Mandarin Chinese in front of a chalkboard on which "Capitalist aggression on Korea" had been written in bold letters and underlined.

The guards applauded like crazy, forcing the POWs to applaud as well. Kim Wong walked around hitting people in the side who weren't applauding loudly enough to show their respect to the revered comrade general.

General Fang exited the stage as Comrade Sun walked on, eyeing the crowd, and taking over the proceedings. The general took a seat to the left of the stage and seemed to revel in the applause, even if it was largely artificial.

After a moment, when the applause had reached an appropriate level, Comrade Sun used his hand to ask the crowd to stop applauding and said, "General Fang welcomes you even though you have been tools of warmongers. The Chinese are now in control of the camps. We will be lenient with those who cooperate, but those who do not will be treated as the war criminals you all are. We call this our leniency policy because we could've executed you. But we chose to spare you in order to teach you the ways of the world. To teach you the ways of Communism. The good students study the truth. But bad students, as well as those who try to escape, will be killed."

A POW tried secretly to boo and hiss. Kim Wong, knowing where the sounds came from, grabbed the man immediately and, nodding to another guard, the two men carried him from the barn.

Comrade Sun smiled and said, "Why not learn from us? Grow and become happy in our camp; that is the answer. Doing the opposite will not get you far."

Two loud shots could be heard right outside the barn. Comrade Sun said, "Applause is good. Booing is for the men who've already given up and don't want to grow and learn but would rather die. The United States' aggression is a good reason for exacting a blood debt. But surrendered soldiers are, nevertheless, treated humanely by the Chinese people's volunteers who will not exact their blood debt, as is their right, providing you show you are willing to learn the truth."

There was a rustling of small movements emanating from the POWs still sat in the ground. For a few it might have been a sign of resignation, for the majority it was a sign of defiance.

☆ ☆ ☆

Over the next few weeks, the Chinese taught many sessions although none of the POWs were happy or really learning anything. Many, however, were beginning to pretend to enjoy the lectures, nodding their heads as if they cared. No one booed or hissed, wanting to avoid being beaten or shot.

When not being lectured to, most of the POWs walked around the camp looking miserable, momentarily pretending to look happier than they were when Comrade Sun or Kim Wong walked by, then hanging their heads and walking on. However, more and more POWs became sick; some simply fell over dead.

Father Kapaun spent a lot of time sneaking around, making warm water for the men to drink, and occasionally bringing them any food he was able to steal. He quietly prayed with the men and prayed silently all the time when alone.

Father Kapaun also joined Doc Anderson in the hospital whenever he could, trying to assist in treating the influx of new cases. The patients were dying faster than they could even acknowledge them.

Father Kapaun and others picked lice off their fellow POWs whenever there was a large breakout of lice infestation, which seemingly came in waves. They shared the meager blankets they'd been given and tried to treat one another's frozen feet.

☆ ☆ ☆

After a couple of weeks, Father Kapaun entered one of the enlisted men's huts and nodded to several POWs who eagerly nodded back, happy to see him at long last. He saw Master Sergeant Bill Richardson, nodded at him, and said, "Hey, Bill" as he sprinkled a tiny amount of tobacco into his pipe and began to puff on it. The tape holding it together was slowly unraveling.

"Where'd you get the tobacco?" Richardson asked.

Father Kapaun nodded at the window, where a soldier called Wang Yu was on guard duty.

"Wang slipped it to me. I'm not supposed to be in the enlisted camp, but Wang lets me through anyway," Father Kapaun answered, handing another bag of tobacco to Bill.

"What's this for?" Richardson asked.

"I could use some help distributing it," Father Kapaun replied.

Richardson took the tobacco, nodded, and said, "I can help, Father."

"Thanks," Father Kapaun said. He hesitated a moment. "You know, we'll need to take action when our troops show up," Father Kapaun said.

"What'd you have in mind?" Richardson asked. He was beginning to doubt their troops even knew where they were, let alone being rescued. He tried not to let the men know how he felt, though he always feared it showed through in his expressions.

"I have a plan," Father Kapaun replied, smiling.

"If the troops don't get here soon, we're going to starve to death," Richardson said.

"That's the first part of my plan: getting us more food," Father Kapaun said, nodding out the window towards Wang.

Wang stood outside, occasionally glancing through the window. Father Kapaun explained that he bounced up and down, pretending to keep warm. Furthermore, under the spot where Wang bounced was a covered hole. Whenever Kim Wong approached the hut, Wang would stop his bouncing and instead nod at Kim Wong as he passed by.

Later that day, outside the enlisted men's hut, with no guards in sight, Father Kapaun and Master Sergeant Bill Richardson pulled off the board that Wang had been bouncing on. He found a cellar underneath.

Father Kapaun stayed on top as Richardson let himself down into the cellar and looked around. It was full of vats of kimchi, a pickled dish of vegetables, mostly cabbage. He looked up at Father Kapaun and said, "Not my favorite food, but my stomach's growling from just looking at it. Thanks, Father. I can take it from here."

Father Kapaun smiled and walked off. Richardson filled two helmet liners full and ran into his hut with them, repeating this action a couple of times, stashing the contents of the helmet liners in a somewhat secure area in the hut. Nothing, of course, was secure from a search by the guards.

Bill began to return for more when he saw Kim Wong and other guards outside near the cellar entrance. He looked at the lid and panicked when he realized he had not closed it completely.

Kim Wong ripped open the lid and disappeared into the cellar. The POWs could hear him cursing in Chinese. Richardson hung his head. How could he be such an idiot? He'd gotten cocky and now his men would pay for it. The other POWs watched as the guards stood around the open hole while Kim Wong investigated.

☆ ☆ ☆

The sun hung low in the sky, a cold pale orange sphere, promising but giving little warmth. Lieutenant Mike Dowe looked into the trash heap and saw Father Kapaun's helmet liner in it. He smiled and said a silent prayer. After a few moments, he turned to walk away and saw Father Kapaun walking towards him.

"How're you doing, Mike?" Father Kapaun asked.

"I've been better," Lieutenant Dowe replied.

"Anything I can do for you, son?"

"Nothing comes to mind, Father. Hey, why'd you toss your helmet liner in there?"

"Well, if I wear it that'll only antagonize the Chinese. Every man who sees it lying in this trash heap is reminded of their God. In fact, it makes me wonder how many silent prayers are said by this old trash heap."

Lieutenant Dowe smiled and said, "Probably more than you'll ever know."

☆ ☆ ☆

The next day, the sun was high and bright, the trash reflecting in the sun. Master Sergeant Richardson tossed some trash into the heap next to Kapaun's helmet liner. He stood there, saying a silent prayer.

After a while, he turned around and saw Kim Wong and two other guards standing nearby.

"You, come," Wong said.

"Me? What did I do?" Richardson asked. He was already starting to sweat in the bleak February sun.

"Yes, you. Come now," Wong said sternly.

The guards started to grab Richardson. He held his hands up, saying, "I can walk on my own."

The guards looked at Kim Wong. He nodded decisively towards Richardson. The guards grabbed his arms in an instant and quickly marched him away.

☆ ☆ ☆

Kim Wong glared down at Master Sergeant Richardson, who was seated next to the two guards in the camp kitchen.

"What's this all about?" Master Sergeant Richardson asked.

"Who took the kimchi?" Wong demanded.

"Your guards took it. Watched them myself. Go check," Richardson protested.

Wong slapped the Master Sergeant in the face and said, "You lie. Tell me now. Nobody eat until you tell me truth."

"Okay. I did it. It was just me," Richardson said.

"No more lies. More do it than just you. I want truth," Wong yelled.

Master Sergeant Richardson sat, silent.

Kim Wong nodded at the guards. The guards tied Richardson's arms behind his back.

"Now, you learn lesson," Kim Wong said.

The guards threw a rope over a truss, pulled Richardson up by his arms until his bare feet were just able to reach the floor. He winced in response to excruciating pain. He felt his shoulders might give out in his already weakened state of health. Then Kim Wong pulled out a baton.

"I'm going to enjoy this," Wong said, smiling sadistically.

Wong struck Bill's feet with the baton repeatedly. Richardson screamed in agony at each impact. Until he could feel nothing more and had no energy to scream.

☆ ☆ ☆

That night, in the enlisted hut, Richardson sat with his back to his men, trying to hide the considerable discomfort he was in and to avoid showing any weakness to his men. Father Kapaun took a seat in front of him and asked, "How'd your talk with Kim Wong go?"

"Well, let's just say we won't be having kimchi anymore," the master sergeant replied gruffly.

Father Kapaun nodded sympathetically. "I've watched the guards, their routine. I know how we can steal more food without getting caught."

PFC Tibor Rubin overheard the conversation, walked over, and took a seat next to the master sergeant.

"Father, isn't one of the ten commandments 'Thou shalt not steal?'" PFC Rubin asked.

Father Kapaun sighed. He looked up. "Oh Lord, forgive us. We ask Saint Dismas, the saint of thieves, to intercede on our behalf so that we may procure enough food to keep our men alive during this trying time."

Richardson grunted his approval.

Tibor smiled at Father Kapaun and said, "You always have the right answer, don't you?"

☆ ☆ ☆

Over the next several days, Father Kapaun worked on stealing food so that the men could keep up their strength, such as it was. He would sneak into a hut with a large sack of potatoes for the men without anyone knowing where it came from.

One day, guards rushed over to break up an argument between POWs, a distraction Father Kapaun used to exit a storage hut with yet more food.

Another day, Father Kapaun, Lieutenant Bill Funchess, and PFC Peter Busatti unloaded bags of soybeans from a boat on the Yalu River, managing to hide one in a bush near the dock that they would return for later.

And on yet another day, Father Kapaun snuck food into the hospital that Doc had renamed "The Death House," feeding a good number of the starving patients. The chaplain knew his duty was to save as many as he possibly could even if it would mean sacrificing himself.

☆ ☆ ☆

On March 2, 1951, Comrade Sun stood on the steps of a bombed-out church, in front of a chalkboard with the words "The Myth of Christianity" written on it. The POWs sat on the steps, watching him as he taught an indoctrination class.

Kim Wong and several other guards surrounded the POWs. Some of the POWs stood holding rocks over their heads as punishment.

☆ ☆ ☆

Later that day, the POWs, seated on the ground, ate a meal that looked and tasted more like birdseed than actual food. Lieutenant Mike Dowe tossed his rations aside. A flock of birds immediately landed and begin eating it, as if to prove his point. He laughed ruefully.

Sergeant Vincent Doyle, seated at the front of the tent, read aloud to the men from a pamphlet.

"Any religious idea, any idea of God at all, any flirtation with God is the most dangerous foulness, the most shameful infection," the sergeant read.

"And who spoke these words?" Comrade Sun asked.

"According to the great doctrines these words came from the noble Stalin, Lenin, the Marx Brothers, and Amos and Andy," he answered, trying to keep a straight face.

Many of the POWs began snickering quietly to themselves so as not to be noticed. Sergeant Doyle tried not to laugh with them. He looked out at the men, cracked a smile, then tried to hide it immediately.

Comrade Sun glanced at the pamphlet, looking extremely confused. He frowned and said, "Lenin is correct. Any religious idea is like a venereal disease. Marx called religion an 'opiate of the masses.' And he called Christianity 'a tool of the bourgeois to keep the proletariat in a state of contentment,' which is why Christianity is a myth. Propaganda for the weak-minded."

Father Kapaun stood and said, "That's a lie. If Christianity is propaganda because it is a myth, then by your own definition the myths you tell of Communism make Communism propaganda as well."

Comrade Sun smirked at Father Kapaun and said, "Thank you for discussing, Kapaun. But you are incapable of proper cognition. We are teaching political education, but you are spreading propaganda against the Communists."

"It's not anti-Communist propaganda, it's Christian love. I shall pray for your soul, Comrade," Father Kapaun said.

"The proletariat has no need for prayer. You cannot see, hear, or feel your God; therefore, he does not exist," Comrade Sun said.

Father Kapaun shook his head and said, "He is as real as the air we breathe. Even though we cannot see the air, we know it is there. Unlike this birdseed you call food. You starve us to death with this crap. Does Communism have no compassion or respect for human life?"

"Why not ask your God to feed you?" Comrade Sun challenged.

Sergeant Doyle stood up and said, "Father's right. This horse manure isn't worth the paper it's printed on!" Shaking his head, he scowled, showing how much he hated everything he'd been reading. He threw the pamphlet on the ground at his feet.

Comrade Sun nodded and the guards rushed over and grabbed Sergeant Doyle. Comrade Sun glared at him and said, "You will be punished severely for your unwarranted cognition."

Lieutenant Funchess stood and yelled, "That's complete crap. On what grounds?"

Comrade Sun smirked at Lieutenant Funchess and said, "For publicly insulting the workers of the Chinese paper-making industry!"

The guards dragged Sergeant Doyle away. The POWs all yelled, standing, and shaking their fists. They were ready for a fight. They'd been ready and this action pushed them over the edge. They started to move toward the entrance. The other guards leveled their rifles at the POWs, forcing them to back down.

Chapter 13

March 16, 1951
Pyoktong, North Korea

That night, Father Kapaun stood at the front of the room in the enlisted hut, trying to cheer up the soldiers. They all looked weary to the bone and ready to give up on the miserable life they were being forced to live.

"We should all pray for Sergeant Vincent Doyle. And on the eve of the day we honor Saint Patrick, we pray for the sustenance to build our bodies and our spirits as we patiently await our liberation from this place by our troops. Amen," Father Kapaun said.

"Amen," everyone responded.

"Well, at least no one can pinch us tomorrow for not wearing green," Lieutenant Ralph Nardella said.

Everyone laughed. Father Kapaun smiled at the lieutenant, pleased that he seemed to have gotten his sense of humor back.

☆ ☆ ☆

The next day the POWs surrounded a horse-drawn cart in the middle of the camp that contained several boxes. Guard Wang Yu jumped from the cart and walked towards Father Kapaun.

PFC Patrick Schuler ripped open a box and pulled out a stack of Communist literature. "Seriously?" he said. "This instead of food?"

"Looks like we finally got a shipment of toilet paper in," Lieutenant Funchess said.

The men laughed and began unloading the boxes from the cart.

Wang Yu looked at Father Kapaun and said, "Father Kapaun. I make confession to you."

"I hope it's not about the tobacco because my men and I ..."

Wang Yu shook his head and said, "No, that was a gift."

Wang pulled up his shirt, revealing a cross around his neck. Father Kapaun made the sign of the cross and said, "God bless you. You are very brave to maintain your faith in God among the Godless. Let's move over there, away from their prying eyes."

Wang Yu nodded and moved with Father Kapaun to a more secluded spot.

"As you know, my name is Wang Yu. I speak some English, but I do not let the officers know for fear they punish me for sympathies towards Western ways."

"Wang, you will have your redemption one day soon. This is the day we honor Saint Patrick," Father Kapaun said.

"I did not know that," Wang said, surprised. He looked very pleased to be hearing this information from him. Wang asked, "Who was this Saint Patrick?"

Father Kapaun smiled and said, "Saint Patrick was enslaved by Irish pirates. Escaped. Became a priest in France and returned to Ireland to convert pagans to Christianity."

"I am truly blessed to hear such truth, Father. The Communists have no truth, only lies they spit out as truth," Wang said.

"Wang, pray with me."

"Yes, Father."

Patrick and Lieutenant Funchess watched Father Kapaun and Wang Yu as they bowed their heads and prayed in a small nearly hidden area. The remaining POWs continued to unload the boxes from the cart, all of them keeping an eye on Wang, looking happy to see a guard praying with Father Kapaun. Maybe God had not deserted them after all.

Father Kapaun stared into the trash heap, looking at his helmet liner laying there upside down as Lieutenant Mike Dowe, Lieutenant Bill Funchess, and PFC Joe Ramirez approached quietly from the direction of the church.

"Penny for your thoughts, Father," Lieutenant Dowe said.

Father Kapaun smiled. "What I'm thinking about is worth a lot more than a penny. I'm thinking about that happy day when the American tanks smash through that fence so I can grab that little S.O.B., Comrade Sun, and kick his little butt right into the Yalu River."

Lieutenant Dowe laughed and said, "You're right, that was worth way more than a penny. If I had a million bucks, I'd just hand it over."

"What is it you used to say ... don't get mad, pray?" PFC Ramirez asked.

"You know Easter is this Sunday," Lieutenant Funchess added.

Father Kapaun nodded, looking back into the trash heap. The moment started to get a little awkward. Dowe, Ramirez, and Funchess looked at each other, wondering what to say next.

"Well, we'll leave you be, Father," Dowe said.

The three men walked off.

Father Kapaun continued to stare into the trash heap. After a while, he reached into the trash heap and pulled out two sticks. He winced, rubbing his leg, looked around the make sure no one was around to see him struggling. He began cleaning the trash off the sticks.

☆ ☆ ☆

On Easter Sunday, March 25, 1951, Father Kapaun walked out of the officers' hut. The sun had barely risen and it was a typically cold morning. He was dressed in his purple priest's stole with a purple ribbon signifying his pastoral office and openly carrying a Catholic missal, a book containing the readings needed to conduct the mass.

When he passed a pair of guards, they did double-takes as Father Kapaun was dressed so differently from what they were used to seeing. They looked at one another confused.

Master Sergeant Bill Richardson and Lieutenant Mike Dowe saw Father Kapaun walking towards the bombed-out church, noticing the slightest of a limp in his walk.

"What's he doing?" the lieutenant asked.

"I think he's about to give an Easter sermon," the master sergeant replied.

Tibor Rubin walked up behind them and said, "If Comrade Sun finds out, he'll probably shoot him in the head before he even gets started."

Other POWs poured out of the tents, following Father Kapaun.

"We can't let that happen," Bill Funchess said.

"Then we better get over there now," Bob Wood added.

"Let's go," Richardson said.

They all followed Father Kapaun, looking concerned about exactly where this was all headed.

Father Kapaun openly defied the atheist Communist ideology by giving an Easter service on the steps of the bombed-out church. Nearly one hundred POWs attended, thrilled at the words, and emboldened by Kapaun's actions. Several guards gathered around, watching the gathering, unsure of what they were supposed to do in a situation like this.

Father Kapaun looked out at the numerous POWs and the guards that stood in front of him and began, "Jesus said to his disciples: 'When the Son of Man comes in his glory, and all the angels with him, he will sit upon his glorious throne, and all the nations will be assembled before him. And he will separate them one from another, as a shepherd separates the sheep from the goats. He will place the sheep on his right and the goats on his left. Then the king will say to those on his right, 'Come, you who are blessed by my Father. Inherit the kingdom prepared for you from the foundations of the world. For I was hungry, and you gave me food, I was thirsty, and you gave me drink, a stranger and you welcomed me, naked and you clothed me, ill and you cared for me, in prison and you visited me.' Then the righteous will answer him and say, 'Lord, when did we see you hungry and feed you, or thirsty and give you drink? When did we see you a stranger and welcome you, or naked and clothe you? When did we see you ill or in prison and visit you?' And the king will say to them in reply, 'Amen, I say to you, whatever you did for one of the least brothers of mine, you did for me.'"

Lieutenant Dowe looked around and saw Father Kapaun's helmet liner upside down in the trash heap.

Father Kapaun continued, saying, "Then he will say to those on his left, 'Depart from me, you accursed, into the eternal fire prepared for the devil and his angels for I was hungry and you gave me no food.'" Father Kapaun looked at the crowd and noticed everyone was hanging on his every word. "'I was thirsty and you gave me no drink, a stranger and you gave me no welcome, naked and you gave me no clothing, ill and in prison, and you did not care for me.'

Then they will answer and say, 'Lord, when did we see you hungry or thirsty or a stranger or naked or ill or in prison, and not minister to your needs?' He will answer them, 'Amen, I say to you, what you did not do for one of these least ones, you did not do for me.' And these will go off to eternal punishment, but the righteous to eternal life. Such is the Gospel of The Lord."

Several guards began to act agitated, worrying what would happen to them if they let Father Kapaun continue. But they looked even more worried about how they were going to stop him.

Father Kapaun said, "As Jesus hung on the cross, he forgave the soldiers who had crucified him, and prayed for his mother and friends. Jesus wanted all of us to be able to live forever with God, so he gave all he had for us. Jesus, let me take a few moments now to consider your love for me. Help me thank you for your willingness to go to your death for me. Help me express my love for you! My Jesus, three hours didst Thou hang in agony, and then die for me; let me die before I sin, and if I live, live for Thy love and faithful service. Our Father ... Hail Mary ... Glory be to the Father. Jesus Christ Crucified."

Everyone called out, "Have mercy on Us."

Father Kapaun paused. He smiled broadly at the crowd. He was proud that he'd been brave enough to come out and preach to his flock. He silently thanked God. Then he said, "May the souls of the faithful departed, through the mercy of God, rest in peace. Amen."

Everyone answered, "Amen."

With the Chinese guards nervously watching, Father Kapaun ended the service by leading the men in song as he started singing "Oh, Beautiful for spacious skies, for amber waves of grain."

The crowd's voices, all in unison, drowned out Father Kapaun as they sang, "For purple mountain majesties, above the fruited plain! America! America! God shed his grace on thee. And crown thy good with brotherhood, from sea to shining sea."

Everyone applauded. The men had never seen Father Kapaun look as happy as he did at that moment.

The singing over, Father Kapaun struggled to make his way through the crowd. Many tearful POWs, grateful for Kapaun's sermon and just as grateful for the song, fought to shake his hand, slap him on the back, or touch him in any way possible.

The guards all looked happy that it was all over, all of them that is except for Wang Yu who hid in the corner, moved to tears himself.

Father Kapaun walked into the officers' hut and collapsed, exhausted. Doc Anderson, who had followed him into the tent, ran over to him.

"Father, are you okay?" Doc Anderson asked.

"Whatever happens, don't let Sun see me like this," Father Kapaun replied.

Doc helped Kapaun onto his bed, lifted his robe, and the pant leg. He stared at Kapaun's leg. After a moment he looked Father Kapaun in the eyes, shook his head, and said, "We need to get you some help now!"

Father Kapaun nodded. He lay quietly as he watched Doc run from the tent.

Chapter 14

March 25, 1951
Pyoktong, North Korea

Doc Anderson and Captain Shadish ran through the hospital, pilfering all of the aspirin and medication they could find. Shadish tried not to look at the patients because every time he did, a look crossed his face that indicated he was doing everything in his power not to vomit.

"This place smells like shit. They call this a hospital?" Shadish said.

"Well, that's what they call it. I call it a Death House," Doc replied. He pocketed some more aspirin.

"I hear that. So, what's happening to Father Kapaun? I'm trying to figure out just how worried I should be," Shadish asked.

"It's his leg, Captain."

"What's wrong with it?"

"It's infected and I believe it has a very large blood clot in it. Clots are visible to the naked eye, but he's got bruising that strongly suggests a clot."

Captain Shadish scowled. "Blood clots aren't something to play around with."

"Exactly. Let's at least get this medicine back to him. I hope this will help," Doc said.

Shadish nodded, still scowling, and said, "I haven't prayed in a long time. It might be about time I got back to it."

"Sure as hell wouldn't hurt," Doc said, pocketing the other medication they'd found.

"You ready?" Doc asked.

"Been ready to leave this place since the moment I entered. Let's go," Shadish responded.

They ran towards the door, Captain Shadish not wanting to look back at the horrors of the place, but unable to erase it from his mind's eye.

☆ ☆ ☆

Doc attended to Father Kapaun in the officers' hut every day. Three weeks had passed with Doc Anderson spending every minute he could trying to get Father Kapaun back on his feet. But it was beginning to look like that would never happen. The only positive thing seemed to be that Comrade Sun had not found out about Father Kapaun's condition yet, which was the thing Father Kapaun feared the most. If Sun discovered he was incapacitated, he'd use it against Father Kapaun's message of God's love. That, Kapaun just couldn't have.

☆ ☆ ☆

It was May 20, 1951. Doc Anderson and Captain Shadish stood outside the officers' hut.

"How's he holding up?" Shadish asked.

Doc shook his head. "Not good. The medicine has helped with the infection, but not enough."

Master Sergeant Bill Richardson, Lieutenant Mike Dowe, PFC Tibor Rubin, PFC Patrick Schuler, PFC Joe Ramirez, Lieutenant Bob Wood, Lieutenant Ralph Nardella, PFC Peter Busatti, Sergeant Pappy Miller, and Sergeant Vincent Doyle all gathered around to hear what was happening.

"Guys, we're trying to have a private conversation here," Captain Shadish told them, trying to get them to leave.

"Whatever's happening to Father Kapaun affects us all," Richardson said.

"Exactly!" Schuler chimed in.

"Yeah, don't hold out on us, Captain," Ramirez added. "He baptized me."

Shadish nodded and said, "Fine. You can stay. Just keep it down. We don't want to attract the attention of the guards."

Shadish turned to Doc and asked, "Doc, how's the blood clot?"

"Blood clot? I didn't know he had a blood clot," Busatti interjected, visibly shocked.

"Quiet," Nardella said, afraid they'd all be forced to leave.

"Yeah, Peter. Shut up or get the hell out of here," Dowe added, wanting to hear everything he could about Father Kapaun's condition.

Busatti nodded, lowered his head, and stayed quiet.

"I had hoped that the medicine would help more, but it turned out to be crap like everything else they have around here. The blood clot will kill him soon if we don't amputate," Doc told the captain.

Many of the soldiers groaned at the thought of amputation.

"I know General Ding-a-ling and Comrade Sun won't allow treatment for him. The guards are checking on him like five times a day. They have to know he's sick," Shadish said.

"I know. Seems like they can't wait for him to die. At least we haven't seen Comrade Sun or Kim Wong in person, but I'm sure the news has gotten back to them. Probably just a matter of time," Doc said.

"You gotta hand it to Kapaun, he gives the troops a pretty firm anchor to hold onto," Shadish said.

Doyle stepped forward, got Doc's attention, and said, "Doc, we have something for Father Kapaun if you could give it to him."

"What is it, Vince?" Doc asked.

"Kimchi," Doyle replied.

Doc laughed, reached out, took the kimchi from the sergeant, and said, "I'll make sure he gets this."

☆ ☆ ☆

Father Kapaun lay in bed in the hut, his leg elevated with a makeshift sling hanging from the ceiling. Lieutenant Funchess attended to him as best he could. He could see that all was hopeless, but he maintained a positive attitude for Kapaun's benefit.

Doc Anderson entered carrying the kimchi Doyle had given him and said to Father Kapaun, "Ready for some kimchi? Courtesy of the men."

Father Kapaun smiled weakly. "They need it more than me, Doc. I'm going to die soon, anyway."

"Don't talk like that," Doc said. He could see that Kapaun was right. The wound was festering to the point of killing him.

Lieutenant Funchess looked into Father Kapaun's eyes and said, "Let me feed you. Get your strength up.

Kapaun responded, "And if I make it through the night, then what?"

To which Doc replied, "Then we'll do what we can to get you through the next day, and the day after that, and the day after that.

Lieutenant Funchess added, "Before you know it, you could be running circles around us all."

Father Kapaun laughed at Lieutenant Funchess. "Using my words against me. All right. Fine."

Father Kapaun nodded at Lieutenant Funchess and allowed him to begin feeding him the kimchi. It had almost no flavor for him. He knew he was near the end of his life. But he also knew what little strength he had should be used to keep the others going.

☆ ☆ ☆

That night, Lieutenant Funchess sat on the floor next to Father Kapaun's cot. They looked through the top of the hut and stared at the full moon. They heard distant gunfire, the booming of heavy artillery.

"The guns sound closer tonight. The Americans are coming. By the next full moon, we'll be free," Father Kapaun said. He was conscious of using the plural pronoun. He wanted Funchess and the others to feel hopeful for themselves, even as he realized his own death was very close. Closer than the approaching guns.

"When I look up at the moon, I wonder if my Sybil is looking up at it, too, thinking of me," Lieutenant Funchess said.

Father Kapaun smiled at him and said, "She is Bill, I'm sure she is. You'll be with her before you know it, and you two will have a long life together. Trust me."

"There's no one I trust more," Lieutenant Funchess said. He reached up and took the father's hand. He lightly squeezed it and then dropped his hand. He had come to respect Kapaun so much that he believed what he said at all times.

They looked back up at the moon, no longer speaking, simply gazing at the moon, each man with a lot on his mind.

☆ ☆ ☆

The next morning, several POWs crowded into the officers' hut, taking a seat or standing anywhere they could. They had been eager to see Father Kapaun. He meant so much to each of them.

Father Kapaun smiled through the pain and shook hands with every man. His own strength was bolstered by the happiness of the men.

"Let me tell you a story," he said. The soldiers all nodded and settled in quietly.

"There was a king who had an old woman brought before him. He told her to renounce her faith or he'd kill her. She refused to renounce her faith. He had her seven sons brought in and threatened to kill them if she didn't obey. She still refused, and he put them to death one by one. The woman cried and the king asked if she was crying because she was sad. She said 'No, they are tears of joy because I know my sons are in heaven.'"

Several of the men, as well as Father Kapaun himself, wiped tears away.

"No one could ever make you renounce your faith," Lieutenant Funchess said to Father Kapaun.

Father Kapaun smiled at the soldiers crowded around. "I know. I'm crying for the same reason the woman did. I'm glad that I am suffering because Our Lord suffered also, and I feel closer to Him. My tears are not tears of pain but tears of joy because I'll be with God soon."

Several of the men spoke at once, telling him he was going to get better, that he couldn't die, that he was needed there, by them, too much.

Before Father Kapaun could respond to the men, Comrade Sun, Kim Wong, and a squad of guards burst into the room.

Captain Shadish looked at them angrily and yelled, "What's the meaning of this?"

"We are taking Kapaun," Kim Wong said.

"No! He's fine where he is!" Lieutenant Funchess argued.

"He goes. Kapaun goes! Now!" Comrade Sun ordered.

A shoving match started. It looked like it was going to get ugly until Father Kapaun motioned for everyone to stop and said, "Take it easy, boys. Tell them back home that I died a happy death."

None of the soldiers wanted to see the Chinese take Father Kapaun. They looked back and forth at each other, wondering what they could do to stop this. But they were weakened by malnutrition and frostbite and sickness. The Chinese had guns, full bellies, and strength on their side.

The guards brought in a stretcher. Lieutenant Dowe looked like he was ready to attack the guards carrying the stretcher.

Father Kapaun saw the hatred in the lieutenant's eyes and said to him, "Mike, don't take it so hard. I'm going where I've always wanted to go. And when I get there, I'll say a prayer for all of you."

Tears began to run down the lieutenant's face as he reluctantly nodded at Father Kapaun.

"If I don't come back, tell my bishop I died a happy death."

The guards grabbed Father Kapaun, manhandled him onto the stretcher, and carried him from the room. Comrade Sun and Kim Wong followed them out the door.

The remaining POWs looked around, not knowing what to do, most of them in tears.

Comrade Sun, looking smug, walked next to Father Kapaun as he was carried on the stretcher. "So now we see what your God can do for you."

Father Kapaun looked up at him and said, "Comrade Sun, please forgive me for all the trouble I've caused you."

Comrade Sun was caught off guard. He stopped and watched as they carried Father Kapaun away, more confused than ever. He heard Father Kapaun say one last thing as they carried him away, "Bless them, O Lord, for they know not what they do."

On May 23, 1951, U.S. Army Chaplin Captain Emil Joseph Kapaun passed from this world.

THE END

Epilogue

Bessie opened the front door of the farmhouse, a smile on her face. Then she saw the man dressed in a military uniform and her face melted.

"Mrs. Kapaun?" the man said. And that was all it took.

"Please, God, no!" Bessie screamed, falling to her knees, crying.

Enos ran out of the barn, immediately understanding the situation. Enos knelt down to comfort Bessie, tears running down his own cheeks as well. Bessie turned to Enos and clutched at him, wailing, as they held each other tightly.

☆ ☆ ☆

Bessie continued to cry in the Kansas graveyard, Enos by her side. She knew Emil was with God, but she wished, despite her faith, that her son had lived. This ceremony seemed empty given that they had no body to bury. Emil had died in that place called Korea and the Army couldn't bring him back. They didn't even know exactly where he was. Taps played as the preacher stood up front, bowing his head. There was a large number of people in attendance including Chaplain Mills, Nurse Mary, and Nurse Deborah, all with tears in their eyes. To each of them, Emil Kapaun had been a selfless friend and advisor. And though they believed he was in heaven; they missed his earthly presence.

Afterword

Father Kapaun had died a few days after being taken away by Comrade Sun and his men. His body was not immediately recovered. Father Kapaun not only served Christians well, but he also served everyone else with equal goodness and kindness. Never thinking of himself, he was always doing something for others.

Bill Richardson, William Funchess, Mike Dowe, Joe Ramirez, Herb 'Pappy' Miller, and many others repatriated and went on to live rich and full lives.

Decades later, Pentagon analysts said Sombokal's POW camp had far fewer deaths of POWs than other camps. Many former POWs claim credit belongs to Father Kapaun's constant efforts to take care of them.

Virtually all POW survivors that were touched by the words or deeds of Father Kapaun, credit him with giving them the moral support and a will to live that lasted another two and a half years after Kapaun's death on May 23, 1951.

For his actions at the Battle of Unsan, Tibor Rubin was awarded the Medal of Honor on Sept. 23, 2005, by President George W. Bush.

Father Kapaun was awarded the Bronze Star with 'V' device and the Distinguished Service Cross for extraordinary heroism in action in Korea, 1950. For his actions at the Battle of Unsan, Father (Captain) Emil J. Kapaun was posthumously awarded the Medal of Honor on April 11, 2013, by President Barack Obama, becoming the most decorated chaplain in U.S. military history.

An estimated 800,000 Chinese troops were killed and nearly 3 million Koreans, a tenth of the entire population, were wounded or killed during the "Forgotten War," 1950 - 1953.

More than 54,000 US soldiers died, over 100,000 were wounded, and 8,179 were Missing-In-Action during the Korean War. Of over 7,000 Prisoners of War taken by North Korean and Chinese Armies — only 3,450 returned, while a staggering 51 percent died in prison camps. Half of all American POWs died in the winter of 1950-51, one of the coldest Korean winters on record. Today there are over 7,500 Americans still MIA from the Korean War.

Kapaun's remains were identified in 2021 and brought back to Kansas.

Father Emil Kapaun was declared a Servant of God by the Roman Catholic Church. The Cause for Canonization for Emil J. Kapaun was begun by the Catholic Diocese of Wichita and once two alleged miracles are confirmed he will be canonized to Sainthood and be the first male Saint born in North America. When canonized, Father Kapaun will become the Patron Saint of POW-MIAs.

About the Author

Jeff Gress is a talented novelist, screenwriter, and movie producer who has been writing for over twenty years.

He recently started his own production company, Landing Hill Pictures, hoping to turn many of his stories and novels into movies or TV series.

Jeff is married with three children and currently living in Las Vegas, Nevada.

Made in the USA
Middletown, DE
25 September 2021

49096622R00142